Parenting adventure - guide for your child's first 5 years

Table of contents

1. welcome to life - the birth of your child

2. the first days - arriving in the new world

3. the first few weeks - your new everyday life

4 The first month - a milestone for parents and child

5. three months old - The baby discovers the world

6 Learning to sleep - a big topic for parents

1. Why your baby isn't sleeping through the night yet
2. Safe sleeping environment: avoid sudden infant death syndrome
3. Develop bedtime rituals
4. Understanding sleep phases: From nap to night sleep
5. What to do if your baby only sleeps in your arms?

7 Six months old - The big leap in development

1. Introducing complementary foods: the right time
2. Breastfeeding or bottle feeding - what changes?
3. The first attempts to sit up
4. How babies learn to eat with their hands
5. Why your baby needs more closeness now

8 Teething - a challenge for parents and child

1. The first teeth: When and how?
2. Symptoms of teething - and how you can help
3. Teething rings, dental gels and home remedies at a glance
4. The right dental care right from the start
5. Teething and sleep problems: What helps?

9. the first year - from baby to toddler

1. The first steps: learning to walk
2. First words and language development
3. Why babies put things in their mouths
4. Playing with mum and dad - why it's so important
5. The first birthday - a special event

10. the defiant phase begins - autonomy and tantrums

1. Why children suddenly say "No!"
2. Understanding and accompanying outbursts of anger
3. Stay patient - tips for stressful moments
4. Loving consistency: setting boundaries
5. The importance of choice

11 The second year of life - motor skills and movement

1. Climbing, running, jumping - the child in motion

2. Why accidents are happening more frequently now

3. Security measures for the home

4. The first wheel and tricycle attempts

5. Promotion of fine motor skills in everyday life

12. language development - how children learn to speak

1. From one-word sentences to small conversations

2. Why your child likes to parrot

3. Books and songs for language development

4. Recognising and acting on speech delays

5. Multilingualism - curse or blessing?

13. getting clean - a big step towards independence

1. When is the right time?

2. Potty training without stress

3. Night nappies - when to do without them?

4. Mastering adversity calmly

5. Reward systems: yes or no?

14. entering the daycare centre - a new world

1. Finding the right daycare centre

2. Gentle familiarisation

3. Overcoming separation anxiety

4. Make your first friends

5. Strengthening daycare centre diseases and the immune system

15. sibling love - from only child to big brother/sister

1. How to prepare your child for a sibling

2. Understanding and accompanying jealousy

3. Time for every child: the balancing act

4. Learning about sibling conflict and reconciliation

5. Shared rituals for sibling bonding

16 The third year - Seeing the world with new eyes

1. Why your child is suddenly questioning everything

3. First friendships: How children socialise

4. Resolving conflicts between children

5. Promoting empathy - why compassion is important

22. media consumption - dealing with television, tablet and co.

1. When is the right time for media?

2. How much screen time is healthy?

3. Select content suitable for children

4. Alternatives to digital media

5. Parents as role models in media consumption

23. promoting independence - small tasks in everyday life

1. Why children want to help

2. Small household chores for preschool children

3. Be patient if it's not perfect

4. Giving freedom of choice: What children can already do

5. The right way to deal with responsibility

24. the first fears - what children worry about

1. Fear of the dark - How you can help

2. Understanding nightmares and night terrors

3. Separation anxiety - How you accompany them

4. Fear of strangers and new situations

5. Conveying trust and security

25. exercise and sport - why activity is so important

1. Romping, climbing, running - understanding the urge to move

2. Which sports are suitable for small children?

3. Promote motor skills through movement games

4. Why children can't sit still

5. Playing outside vs. playing inside

26. storytelling - the magic of fantasy

1. Why children love stories

2. Storytelling, reading aloud or audio books?

3. Encourage creativity through your own stories

1. welcome to life - the birth of your child

The birth of a child is a magical moment - a unique, overwhelming and deeply emotional event. After months of anticipation, perhaps also uncertainty and tension, you finally hold your baby in your arms. This first moment is unforgettable - a little person enters the world, and with him or her the adventure of parenthood begins for you.

1.1 The magic of the first few hours

The first few hours after the birth are characterised by a very special atmosphere. Your baby comes from a warm, safe environment into a completely new world. The lights are brighter, the noises louder, the air cooler. But one thing remains the same: your closeness.

Many babies are surprisingly alert in the first few minutes after birth. They blink, look around and seem to search for familiar faces with their eyes. They can already see at a short distance - so they recognise your face, especially when you talk to them.

This moment is precious for you as a family. Your baby is now here and you will slowly get to know him or her. The first cuddles, the first conscious awareness of your little fingers, the warmth of your baby's tummy on your skin - these are all memories that will last forever.

1.2 Skin-to-skin contact: Why it is so important

A newborn not only has physiological needs such as warmth and food, but also a deep desire for closeness and security. Skin-to-skin contact, often referred to as "bonding", plays a crucial role.

Immediately after birth, the baby is placed on mum's (or dad's) bare chest if possible. This contact helps the baby to get used to the new environment. Its temperature, breathing and even heartbeat can be regulated by your closeness.

Studies show that babies who have a lot of physical contact with their parents in the first few hours are calmer, drink better and develop a closer bond with their parents later on. Cuddling also has benefits for you: Skin-to-skin contact releases the hormone oxytocin, which stimulates your milk production and strengthens the emotional bond with your baby.

If medical intervention is needed and you can't hold your baby immediately, dad can step in. Skin-to-skin contact with dad is just as valuable and can help the baby feel safe.

1.3 The first cry - communication begins

Your baby's first cry is a moving moment. After nine months in the womb, it fills its lungs with air for the first time. The first cry shows that your baby is breathing and is ready to arrive in this new world.

But crying is not just a sign of breathing, it is also the first form of communication. Babies cry for many reasons - hunger, tiredness, cold, excessive demands. You will soon learn to distinguish between the different cries and understand what your baby is trying to tell you.

A little tip: Many parents feel helpless at first when their baby cries. But over time, you will develop a feeling for your child's needs. Stay calm, comfort your baby and trust in your growing bond.

1.4 The first breast or bottle feed

Shortly after birth, the first feeding begins - either through breastfeeding or with a bottle. Most babies have a natural sucking reflex after birth and intuitively look for the breast.

Breastfeeding for the first time can take a little practice. Some babies suckle vigorously straight away, others need a little longer to get used to the breast. It's perfectly normal if it doesn't work straight away at first. A breastfeeding counsellor or midwife can help you find the right position and ensure that your baby is latched on well.

If you don't want to or can't breastfeed, a bottle is a good alternative. The most important thing is that your baby is full and satisfied - whether through breast milk or formula milk.

A few tips for the first meal:

- Be patient and give yourselves time to get used to each other.

- Make sure you are in a comfortable position so that breastfeeding or feeding is comfortable for you.

- Your baby only needs small amounts of milk in the first few days - a newborn's stomach is tiny.

- If your baby has difficulty drinking, ask a midwife or breastfeeding counsellor for help.

1.5 Emotional rollercoaster: the parents' feelings

The birth of your child is an emotional milestone - and with this joy often comes unexpected feelings. Many new parents experience a mixture of happiness, relief, exhaustion and sometimes uncertainty in the first few hours.

It's completely normal to feel overwhelmed. After giving birth, your hormone balance changes and this can lead to tears of joy, but also to inexplicable mood swings. Mums in particular often experience the so-called "baby blues" - a short phase in which they feel sad or overwhelmed for no apparent reason.

Fathers also have strong emotions. Suddenly there is this little being for whom they are responsible. Some feel a deep connection straight away, others need a little time to grow into their new role.

What helps during this time?

- **Talk to each other:** Talk to your partner or midwife about your feelings. Everything you feel is normal.

- **Get some rest:** Sleep is precious in the first few days. Try to relax when your baby is sleeping.

- **Accept help:** Family or friends can support you - be it with a cooked meal or simply with an open ear.

- **Don't expect too much of yourself:** No one is a perfect parent from the start. It's a learning process, and that's perfectly fine.

Conclusion: A new phase of life begins

The birth of your baby marks the beginning of a new era. In these first few hours, a close bond develops between you and your child and you start to get to know each other. Everything is new - for your baby, but also for you as a parent.

Take your time, enjoy the moment and don't forget: you don't have to be perfect. Your baby doesn't need perfect parents, it just needs you - with all your love, care and warmth. 🖤

2. the first days - arriving in the new world

After the birth, an exciting but also challenging time begins for your baby - and for you. The first few days after the birth are characterised by many changes, new routines and a lot of emotions. While your baby gets used to life outside the womb, you learn to deal with your new role as a parent.

These days are unique - full of magical moments, but also uncertainties. Don't worry, you will grow with the task and your baby will show you what it needs. Here you can find out what is particularly important in the first few days after the birth.

2.1 The first nappy change

Changing a nappy for the first time - a small challenge for many new parents. Your hands may be shaking, the baby is kicking and the tiny nappy doesn't quite want to fit. But don't worry: after a few days, changing nappies becomes routine.

Newborn babies have a very special type of faeces in the first few days: so-called meconium. It is black, sticky and reminiscent of tar. This can be irritating at first, but is completely normal. After a few days, when your baby has ingested colostrum (the first milk) or infant milk, the faeces will become softer and lighter in colour.

Tips for nappy changes:

- **Have everything to hand:** Wet wipes, fresh nappy, possibly a wound protection cream.
- **Safety first:** Always hold your baby with one hand, especially when lying on the changing table.
- **Clean gently but thoroughly:** For girls in particular, make sure to wipe from front to back to avoid infection.
- **Allow air to reach the bum:** A few minutes without a nappy helps to avoid skin irritation.

Sometimes a sore bottom can occur. In this case, let your baby kick without a nappy more often and use a wound protection cream with zinc.

2.2 Bonding with mum and dad

In the first few days after birth, the bond between parent and child is particularly important. Your baby recognises your voice and your smell - it already knows that you are its secure base.

Bonding means establishing a deep emotional connection. Skin contact, cuddling and quiet moments help with this. It is just as important for fathers to build closeness from the very beginning.

What promotes bonding?

- Lots of skin-to-skin contact (kangaroo method)

- Gentle speaking or humming

- Eye contact and smile

- Slow, calm rocking on the arm

If you have had a caesarean section or were unable to hold your baby straight away for other reasons, there is no need to worry. Bonding can also be intensively built up over the next few days and weeks.

2.3 Why newborns sleep so much

You may have already wondered: Your baby sleeps an incredible amount! Newborns sleep up to 16-18 hours a day, but in short periods. Their sleep rhythm is not yet adapted to day and night.

A lot of sleep is necessary because your baby's brain processes so many new impressions. It even learns while it sleeps. However, the irregular sleep rhythm can be stressful for parents.

Tips for a better sleep rhythm:

- **Distinguish between day and night:** during the day it can be brighter and a little louder, but at night it can be dark and quiet.

- **Establish a gentle bedtime ritual:** For example, soft humming, gentle rocking or a quiet music box.

- **Not too many stimuli before sleep:** too much action just before your baby falls asleep can overwhelm them.

If your baby only sleeps in your arms, this is completely normal. It has felt your closeness for months and only feels really safe this way. You can try to slowly get him used to his cot, but don't force it.

2.4 Crying as an expression - what your baby is telling you

Crying is the only way for newborn babies to communicate. Some babies cry very little, others more. But every baby cries for a specific reason.

Common reasons for crying:

- Hunger

- Full nappy

- Tiredness

- Overload

- Need for closeness

Some parents worry that their baby is crying too much. But in the first few days, crying does not mean that something is wrong. Your baby first has to get used to the new world.

A few tips to calm you down:

- Carry your baby in your arms or in a baby carrier. Movement calms you down.

- Speak softly or sing to him. Your voice will sound familiar.

- Wrap your baby in a light blanket (swaddling) to remind him of the tightness in his stomach.

- Turn on "white noise", e.g. the sound of a hairdryer or hoover - this imitates the sounds of the womb.

If your baby seems inconsolable or cries continuously, it may have wind or be unwell. Gentle tummy rubs or a relaxing cuddle can help.

2.5 Postpartum visit: dos and don'ts

After the birth, many family members look forward to getting to know the baby. But the first few days are a sensitive time - for you, your baby and your partner.

Dos:
✓ Ask in advance if and when a visit is desired.
✓ Keep the visit short (30-60 minutes is enough).
✓ Bring a snack instead of expecting to be entertained.
✓ Wash your hands before holding the baby.

Don'ts:
✗ Turn up unannounced.
✗ Expecting to be allowed to hold the baby immediately.
✗ Overwhelming parents with well-meaning but unsolicited advice.
✗ Stay overtime - mum and dad need peace and quiet.

You can say without a guilty conscience: "It's not suitable today." Your well-being and that of your baby take priority.

Conclusion: A new beginning for all of you

The first few days with your baby are a phase of adjustment - for both of you. You learn to understand your baby and your baby gets used to life outside the womb.

There are many wonderful moments - the first eye contact, the first quiet chuckle. But there are also challenging times - sleepless nights, insecurities, tears. All of this is normal.

💡 **Always remember that:**

- You don't have to be perfect - your baby just needs you as you are.

- It's okay to ask for help when you're exhausted.

- Every day brings new surprises - enjoy them.

The first few days are like a gentle introduction to the adventure of parenthood. Stay patient, take your time - and above all: have faith in yourself! 🤍

3. the first few weeks - your new everyday life

After the first exciting days, a new everyday life with your baby slowly begins. But this everyday life is anything but ordinary - it changes almost daily. Your baby is growing, learning and developing at breakneck speed. At the same time, you as a parent are also learning a lot: How your baby signals hunger, which noises calm it down and why it sometimes whines for seemingly no reason.

These first few weeks can be wonderful, but also exhausting. Lack of sleep, uncertainty and constantly being there for a tiny human are a big adjustment. But don't worry - with a little patience and composure, you'll find your own rhythm.

3.1 The rhythm between breastfeeding and sleeping

One of the first things you will learn in these weeks is that a newborn baby does not (yet) have a fixed rhythm. Instead of a regular daily routine, your baby decides when to drink, sleep and be awake. This can be challenging for parents because their own needs often have to be put on the back burner.

Babies have small stomachs and therefore need to feed frequently - often every two to three hours. Especially in the first few weeks, it can feel like you are breastfeeding or giving bottles around the clock. This is completely normal!

Tips for a relaxed breastfeeding or bottle-feeding period:

- **Don't let yourself get stressed:** Your baby will drink for as long as it needs.

- **Look out for signs of breastfeeding:** A baby looking for the breast or sucking its fingers is hungry - often before it cries.

- **Create a pleasant atmosphere:** A quiet place with a comfortable armchair or cushion can help.

- **Be aware that the rhythm comes with time:** after around six to eight weeks, babies often start to drink and sleep more regularly on their own.

Sleep also changes. Newborns sleep a lot, but in short periods. Most fall asleep again after one or two hours because they have not yet become accustomed to day and night. During this time, it can help to keep the rooms bright and active during the day, but darker and quieter at night.

3.2 Growth spurts: why your baby is changing

Many parents notice sudden changes in their baby's behaviour in the first few weeks. A baby who was sleeping peacefully yesterday is now cranky and constantly wants to be carried. This is often due to a growth spurt.

In the first three months, your baby goes through several developmental leaps in which it learns new skills. These spurts can be accompanied by increased crying, less sleep and increased hunger.

What happens during a growth spurt?

- Your baby suddenly notices more - sounds, light, touch.

- It wants more closeness because the world suddenly seems strange to it.

- It drinks more frequently to get the extra energy it needs.

How can you help?

- Be patient and give your baby lots of closeness.

- Carrying often helps - many babies calm down in a baby carrier or sling.

- Remember: these phases are exhausting, but they will pass. Afterwards, your baby will often be able to do something new, for example hold their head better or grasp more purposefully.

3.3 Baby massage and touch for security

Babies love touch - it gives them a sense of security, safety and closeness. Baby massages are a wonderful way to soothe your baby and strengthen the bond.

How does a baby massage work?

- Use a warm, skin-friendly oil (e.g. almond oil).

- Gently massage your arms, legs and stomach with circular movements.

- Pay attention to your baby's signals - if it gets restless, take a break.

- Gentle abdominal massages in particular can help with flatulence.

Massages are not only relaxing for your baby, but also for you as a parent. They offer a valuable opportunity to consciously spend time together and get to know your baby's signals better.

3.4 The first visits to the doctor and U examinations

In the first few weeks, you will have a few visits to the doctor. These are important to check whether your baby is developing well.

Typical examinations during this time are

- **The U2 (3rd-10th day of life):** The baby is thoroughly examined here - weight, reflexes, skin colour and drinking behaviour.

- **The U3 (4th-5th week):** Here, particular attention is paid to hip development, as some babies may have hip dysplasia.
- **Vitamin D administration:** Babies are often given vitamin D drops to support bone health.

Many parents are nervous about these examinations. If you have any questions, write them down beforehand - doctors and midwives will be happy to help you.

3.5 Parenting as a team - communication between partners

The first few weeks with a baby are wonderful, but they can also be a stress test for the relationship. Lack of sleep, new responsibilities and insecurities can lead to both parents feeling overwhelmed.

How do you stay strong as a team?

- **Talk about your feelings:** It's normal to feel overwhelmed sometimes. Talk about it openly.
- **Divide up the tasks:** Even if one parent is breastfeeding, the other can swaddle, soothe or simply offer support.
- **Don't expect too much:** nobody has to be a "perfect" parent. Small mistakes are part of it.
- **Take time for yourself:** Even if it's just a hot shower or half an hour of relaxation - self-care is important.

Fathers or non-breastfeeding partners in particular can sometimes feel superfluous because the baby is so attached to mum. But they are also extremely important: a baby needs the love and closeness of both parents. Small rituals such as a daily cuddle or being carried together help to strengthen the bond.

Conclusion: A new everyday life full of changes

The first few weeks are a time of getting to know each other, of growing - for your baby and for you.

What you can take with you:

- It's normal if you sometimes feel insecure. All parents learn over time.
- Your baby is developing quickly and every day brings new little miracles.
- Growth spurts and restless phases will pass - patience and closeness will help your baby.
- Take care of yourself and your relationship - parenting is teamwork.

These first few weeks are challenging, but they are also a unique and wonderful time. Enjoy the moments with your baby - even if they are sometimes chaotic! 🤍

4 The first month - a milestone for parents and child

Congratulations! Your baby is now one month old and you have mastered the first few weeks as a new parent. It has probably been an exciting time full of new experiences, emotions and challenges. Perhaps you now feel a little more confident in your new role, or perhaps you are still struggling with insecurities - both are completely normal!

The first month marks an important milestone in your baby's development. It starts to become more aware of you, its senses become sharper and small steps forward become noticeable. A lot changes for you as parents too: everyday life slowly becomes more routine and you learn to understand your baby better and better.

Let's take a closer look at these exciting developments.

4.1 Your baby starts to become aware of you

In the first few weeks, your baby was still very preoccupied with itself. It had to get used to its new surroundings, sleep and drink a lot. But now it is starting to become more aware of its surroundings - and you in particular!

Your baby recognises your face and your voice. It can't see very far yet, but as you approach it, it will fix its eyes on you for longer and longer. You may also notice that it becomes calmer when you speak or sing - it feels safe and secure because it recognises your voice from its time in the womb.

How can you support your baby during this phase?

- Talk to him a lot, even if he doesn't answer yet. Your baby loves your voice!

- Hold it in your arms often and look it in the eye. This eye contact promotes bonding.

- Respond to his sounds and facial expressions - this will teach him that communication is a beautiful thing.

4.2 Development of the senses: seeing, hearing, feeling

Babies are born with amazing abilities, but their senses develop gradually.

👀 **See:**

- Your baby is best at recognising contrasts. That's why black and white patterns or strong colour combinations fascinate them.

- It can't see very far yet, but it can recognise your face from about 20-30 cm away.

- In this month, it begins to consciously direct its gaze towards objects or people and follow them with its eyes.

👂 **Listen:**

- Your baby reacts particularly to your voice - it has a calming effect.

- Sudden, loud noises can startle it.

- Soft music or the humming of a melody can calm it down.

Feel:

- Your baby loves being touched and gently stroked.

- Cuddling, massages and skin contact are important for emotional development.

- It slowly begins to discover his hands and put them in its mouth.

Tip: Hang a black and white card with patterns next to the changing table or slowly move a toy back and forth in front of your baby's eyes. You'll see how he starts to look at it!

4.3 The first small attempt at a smile

One of the best moments for parents: the first conscious smile!

Babies smile in their sleep right from birth - this is known as an "angel's smile". But after around four to six weeks, many babies show their first real smile. It is their first conscious reaction to you and a sign that they recognise you and are happy.

This smile is not only incredibly cute, but also an important developmental step. It shows that your baby can process social signals.

How can you encourage the first smile?

- Often look directly at your baby while you are talking to him.

- Smile at it - babies often mimic facial expressions.

- Play gentle games like "peek-a-boo".

And don't worry if your baby takes a little longer to smile - every child develops at their own pace.

4.4 Why the prone position is important

An important developmental step in this month is the prone position. Even if many babies don't like it at first, it is important that they lie on their tummy regularly.

Why?

- The prone position strengthens the neck, back and shoulder muscles.

- It prepares your baby to lift its head and turn later on.

- It helps to avoid a flat head shape, which can be caused by lying on your back for long periods.

Tips for a pleasant tummy time:

- Start with short sessions of 1-2 minutes, several times a day.

- Place your baby on your chest - this will make him feel safe and encourage him to lift his head.

- Use an interesting toy or a little mirror to arouse his interest.

- Make the tummy time a game and not a chore - if your baby is unhappy, pick them up and try again later.

Over time, your baby will become stronger and better able to hold its head. Soon it will start to look around curiously!

4.5 Your body after the birth - recovery and regression

As your baby grows and develops, your body also undergoes a major change. Many mums underestimate how long it takes to recover from childbirth.

In the first few weeks you may still feel afterpains, especially when breastfeeding. Your belly is still soft and the uterus is slowly receding. You may feel tired or emotional - your body needs time to adjust.

What helps with recovery?

- **Postnatal exercises:** Start gently with pelvic floor exercises as soon as your doctor or midwife gives the green light.

- **Allow rest:** Sleep when your baby sleeps - even if it's hard.

- **Healthy diet:** Drink plenty of water and eat nutritious meals to keep you energised.

- **Accept support:** Get help around the house and accept any help offered.

This time can also be emotionally challenging. The so-called "baby blues" can occur - a phase in which you feel sad or overwhelmed for no apparent reason. If these feelings persist, talk to your midwife or a doctor. You are not alone!

Conclusion: The first month - an adventure full of little wonders

The first month is a time of getting to know you, growing and marvelling. Your baby starts to become aware of you, develops its senses and may even give you its first smile. At the same time, you are learning to master your new everyday life as a parent - with all its ups and downs.

💡 What you can take with you:

- Your baby recognises you and feels safe with you. Your closeness is the most important thing for its development.

- The prone position helps to strengthen the muscles - but always playfully and without pressure.

- Your baby will slowly start to send social signals - be it by smiling or chatting for the first time.

- Your body needs time to recover - be patient with yourself.

Even if the days are sometimes exhausting: Enjoy the little moments. Your baby is growing faster than you think - and this first month is a unique time that you will never experience again. 🩶

5. three months old - The baby discovers the world

Your baby is now three months old - a real milestone! It has made incredible progress in these first few weeks. They are more attentive, interact more consciously with their environment and are beginning to discover the world around them with curiosity.

You may have the feeling that your baby is now communicating with you more "properly": It smiles at you, responds to your voice and even starts to make sounds. His movements are also becoming more controlled - he reaches for things, watches his hands and kicks happily when he is happy.

In this chapter, you will find out about the exciting developments your baby is making this month and how you can support them through play.

5.1 Grasping, feeling, discovering - motor skills develop

At three months, your baby begins to use their hands more consciously. Whereas in the first few weeks it still made uncontrolled reflex movements, it now looks specifically at its fingers and starts to reach for things.

💡 **What happens now?**

- Your baby watches his hands and fingers with fascination - they are his first "toys".
- It opens and closes its hands purposefully and tries to grasp objects.
- Hand-eye coordination improves: the child looks at an object and tries to touch it.
- When it gets hold of something, it holds on to it - often things go straight into its mouth!

How can you support your baby?

- Offer him different materials to feel - soft fabrics, smooth wooden rings or crackling cloths.
- Hold a toy in front of its face and move it slowly back and forth so that it follows with its eyes.
- Give him soft rattles or grasping toys to hold - this strengthens his muscles and trains his senses.

Grasping is one of the most important skills in development - these small, playful attempts later become targeted movements such as eating with a spoon or colouring with pencils.

5.2 Why babies start to "chat"

Another exciting highlight this month: your baby is starting to speak out loud! It is no longer just making random noises, but is consciously experimenting with its voice.

What is changing this month?

- Your baby starts to gurgle, coo and babble ("Aaaah", "Eeeh", "Oooo").
- It reacts to your voice - when you speak to it, it responds with sounds.
- It "chats" with its own hands or toys.
- It squeaks with joy or hums when it is concentrated.

This is how you can encourage your baby:

- **Talk to him a lot!** Tell him what you are doing ("Now I'll put your jacket on").
- **Respond to his "babbling".** When it says "Aaaah", repeat it - this shows it that communication is a back and forth process.
- **Sing songs to him.** Babies love melodies and often begin to imitate sounds.

These "conversations" are the first step in language development. Even if it doesn't sound like real words yet - your baby is practising to speak!

5.3 The magic of mirroring: baby's reactions

Babies love faces - and especially their own! You may have noticed that your baby looks in the mirror with fascination. It doesn't recognise itself yet, but it loves the movements and facial expressions it sees.

What is happening here?

- Your baby observes faces closely and begins to imitate them.
- It smiles when it looks in the mirror (and sees you in the background).
- It starts to react to facial expressions - if you smile, it smiles back!

Play with your baby:

- Hold it in front of a mirror and make funny faces.
- Move the mirror slightly - your baby will be amazed!
- Make a movement, e.g. stick out your tongue - your baby may try to imitate it.

These first social interactions are important for emotional and cognitive development. Your baby learns by observing and imitating - a skill that they will need later when speaking and socialising.

5.4 Baby carrier or pushchair? Advantages and disadvantages

Parents are often faced with the question: Should I rather push my baby in a pram or carry them in a baby carrier? Both options have advantages and disadvantages - the best solution is often a mixture of both.

Baby carrier or sling:

☑ Promotes bonding - your baby feels safe and secure.

☑ Helps with wind and colic because it is carried in an upright position.

☑ Practical for travelling when paths are uneven or there is a lot going on.

☑ Hands remain free for other things.

✖ Can be tiring to carry for long periods of time.

✖ In summer it can get warm when baby and parents are close together.

Pushchair:

☑ Ideal for longer walks - less strain on the parent's back.

☑ Baby can lie flat and sleep.

☑ Well suited for shopping or if you want to transport extra things.

✖ Less proximity to the baby - it can sometimes feel restless.

✖ Not always practical for stairs or rough paths.

Tip: Try out what works best for you and your baby. Many parents use a baby carrier at home and a pushchair for walks.

5.5 The first growth spurt - what you need to know

Around the third month, many babies go through a significant growth spurt. You may notice that your baby suddenly …

- **cries more or is fussy**

- **wants to drink more often** (breastfeeding children demand the breast more often)

- **sleeps worse or is more restless**

Why is this happening?

Your baby is not only growing physically, but is also making a big leap mentally. It is much more aware of its surroundings and processes new impressions.

How can you support your baby during this time?

- Give more closeness: Carrying, cuddling and reassuring words help.

- Offer breast or bottle feeds on demand - your baby needs more energy now.

- Be patient - this phase will pass, and afterwards your baby will often be able to do something new!

After this phase, your baby will often be much more awake, active and attentive. It may start to move more purposefully or "talk" for longer periods of time.

Conclusion: A great leap in development!

The third month brings many exciting changes: Your baby begins to grasp, chat, imitate faces and perceive the world more actively.

What you can take with you:

- Your baby is starting to use his hands purposefully - give him opportunities to discover them.

- Communication is particularly important now - talk to your baby a lot!

- Closeness and carrying help to soothe and nurture your baby.

- Growth spurts can be exhausting - but they mean great leaps in development.

The first three months are over - your baby is no longer a newborn, but a small being that actively interacts with its environment. The next few months will be even more exciting - your baby is well on the way to becoming a little world explorer! 🚀 🤍

6 Learning to sleep - a big topic for parents

Sleep is one of the key issues in the first year of a baby's life - and often one of the biggest challenges for parents. In the first few months, babies sleep a lot, but not necessarily when their parents would like them to. An uninterrupted night's sleep? Most babies are still a long way from that.

Perhaps you have already asked yourself: Why does my baby only sleep in short stages? Why does he wake up so often? And above all: What can I do to help him sleep better?

In this chapter, you will find out why babies sleep differently to adults, how you can create a safe and comfortable sleeping environment and which gentle methods you can use to help your baby fall asleep.

6.1 Why your baby isn't sleeping through the night yet

Many parents wonder when their baby will finally "sleep through the night". But what does "sleeping through the night" actually mean? In the first few months, a sleep period of five to six hours is already considered "sleeping through the night". An eight-hour night's sleep is still a dream of the future for most babies.

Why do babies wake up so often?

- **Their sleep cycle is shorter:** an adult goes through sleep phases of around 90 minutes, a baby only 45-60 minutes. This means they wake up more often.

- **It needs to eat regularly:** A small stomach needs frequent meals, especially in the first few months.

- **Sleeping is a matter of maturation:** a baby's brain develops rapidly - regular, deep sleep comes with time.

- **Developmental leaps can influence sleep:** Growth spurts, new abilities or external stimuli can cause restless nights.

Tip: It is completely normal for your baby not to sleep like an adult in the first few months. Be patient - his sleeping behaviour will mature over time.

6.2 Safe sleeping environment: preventing sudden infant death syndrome

The safety of your baby during sleep is the most important thing. Research shows that a few simple measures can significantly reduce the risk of sudden infant death syndrome (SIDS).

☑ **You should do that:**

- Always lay your baby on their **back** to sleep.
- The baby should sleep in **its own cot**, but preferably in the parents' bedroom.
- A firm **mattress without pillows, blankets or cuddly toys** is ideal.
- The temperature in the room should be **between 16-18°C** - not too warm.
- Use a **sleeping bag** instead of a blanket so that the baby's face is not covered.
- **Avoid cigarette smoke** - both before and after the birth.

✖ **You should avoid this:**

- Let it sleep on its stomach (unless it is awake and under supervision).
- Soft bedding, nest or pillow in the cot.
- Overheating - clothing that is too warm or heaters increase the risk.
- Sleeping together in the parents' bed can be dangerous if pillows or blankets could cover the baby.

A safe place to sleep gives you as parents a reassuring feeling and ensures that your baby can sleep soundly.

6.3 Developing bedtime rituals

Babies love rituals - they give them security and help them to understand the day-night rhythm. A gentle bedtime ritual can help your baby to calm down and adjust to the night.

✦ **Gentle bedtime rituals can be:**

- **A warm bath** in the evening (not necessarily every day, but as a quiet ritual).
- **A gentle massage** with baby oil to promote relaxation.
- **A quiet playtime**, followed by cuddling.
- **Singing or humming softly** to lull the baby to sleep.
- **One last breastfeeding or** bottle-feeding **moment** to provide a sense of security.

💡 **Important:** Make sure that the environment is quiet. Televisions, loud music or too much light can overstimulate the baby.

Over time, your baby will recognise the sequence of the ritual and adjust to the fact that it is now bedtime.

6.4 Understanding sleep phases: From nap to night sleep

Babies have different sleep patterns to adults. They spend more time in the light sleep phase, in which they can easily wake up. This has an evolutionary advantage: in early times, deep sleep meant greater danger.

Typical sleep patterns of a baby at three to six months:

- A total of **14-17 hours of sleep per day**.

- **Several naps** a day, usually 3-4 short sleep phases.

- **Longer sleep phases** at night, but no continuous night's sleep yet.

- Some babies fall asleep easily, others need longer and more support.

How you can help:

- Find out when your baby is tired - yawning, rubbing eyes or restlessness are signs.

- Keep a **consistent daily routine** - regular sleeping times help the baby to find its rhythm.

- Your baby must not be **overtired**, otherwise it will be more difficult to fall asleep.

6.5 What to do if your baby only sleeps in your arms?

Many babies sleep best in your arms, in a carrier or while breastfeeding. This is completely normal - after all, your baby has spent nine months in the safety of your arms.

But if you can't carry your baby all day or want to slowly get them used to their own bed, there are gentle ways:

Gradually get used to your own bed:

1. **First rock him to sleep, then lay him in his cot** (quietly with your hand on his tummy).

2. **Put a worn T-shirt in bed** (so it smells like you).

3. **Work with quiet noises** (quiet "white noise" or heartbeat noises have a calming effect).

4. **Gently lay** it **back down again and again when it wakes up** - babies need time to get used to this.

Important:

- Don't force it! If your baby is inconsolable, take it out again and try again later.

- Many babies only learn to fall asleep without physical contact over time. Be patient!

Conclusion: Sleeping is a learning process - for your baby and for you

A baby's sleep is a great adventure - with ups and downs. But don't worry: your baby will learn to sleep longer over time.

What you can take with you:

✓ Babies sleep differently to adults - waking up frequently is normal.

✓ A **safe sleeping environment** is essential for healthy sleep.

✓ **Bedtime rituals** help to ring in a peaceful night.

✓ Every baby develops their own sleep rhythm - patience is required.

✓ Closeness is important - but you can gently acclimatise your baby to their own bed.

Even if it can be exhausting: Your baby doesn't sleep badly - it just sleeps like a baby! Everything will settle down over time. And until then? Use every quiet minute for little moments of relaxation - you're doing a great job!

7 Six months old - The big leap in development

Your baby is now six months old - an incredible journey lies behind you! In these six months, your baby has developed from a tiny newborn into a small, active explorer. This is the start of a particularly exciting phase: your baby is becoming more and more mobile, is starting to become even more aware of its surroundings and may even be ready for its first solid food.

In this chapter, you will find out what big developmental leaps your baby is making now, how you can support it and what changes you can expect in the coming weeks.

7.1 Introducing complementary foods: the right time

A big topic in the sixth month is complementary feeding. Many parents ask themselves: When is the right time to start solid foods?

The World Health Organisation (WHO) recommends exclusively breastfeeding or giving infant milk for the first six months. After that, complementary foods can be introduced gradually.

Signs that your baby is ready for complementary food:

✓ It can sit upright with support.

✓ It shows interest in your food, watches you eat or reaches for your plate.

✓ They can move food backwards with their tongue (no longer reflexively pushing it out with their tongue).

✓ They can grasp things purposefully and bring them to their mouth.

If your baby is not yet showing these signs, it's better to wait a few more weeks - every child develops at their own pace.

How you can get started:

- Start with simple, easily digestible foods such as carrot, pumpkin or parsnip porridge.

- Let your baby have a say - if it pushes the spoon away or turns away, it may not be ready yet.

- Solid food is a supplement, not a substitute meal - breastfeeding or bottle feeding remains important.

As an alternative to porridge, you can also try baby-led weaning (BLW) - this involves giving your baby soft, bite-sized pieces of food that they can grab and put in their mouth themselves.

7.2 Breastfeeding or bottle feeding - what changes?

Even when complementary foods are introduced, breast milk or infant milk remains the main food. Your baby still needs milk for important nutrients and energy.

What is changing now:

- Breastfed children may demand the breast a little less often because they are fuller for longer due to the complementary food.

- Bottle-fed children may drink a little less, depending on how much solid food they are already eating.

- Some babies prefer small amounts of solid food at the beginning and continue to stick to their milk.

Important: Don't force your baby to eat. It is completely normal if your baby drinks more from the breast or bottle on some days and tries more solid foods on other days.

7.3 The first attempts to sit up

Another milestone is just around the corner: your baby is getting stronger and stronger and may already be starting to pull himself forwards from the supine position or support himself with his arms.

What happens now?

- Many babies try to push themselves up with their arms when lying on their tummy.

- Some babies roll onto their side and try to sit up from there.

- If your baby pulls on your hands, it can sometimes sit up briefly - but not yet on its own.

How can you help?

- Encourage your baby to play in the prone position - this strengthens the muscles.

- Do not sit your child down artificially (e.g. propped up with a cushion) if it cannot yet get into position itself.

- Play with him in a slightly upright position (e.g. on your lap) to strengthen his muscles.

Soon the time will come: Your baby will be sitting up by himself - a huge step in his development!

7.4 How babies learn to eat with their hands

Food is not just food - it's an experience! Many babies are now beginning to explore food not only with their mouths but also with their hands.

What happens now?

- Your baby reaches for food and tries to put it in his mouth himself.
- It crushes food with its fingers - an important learning process for fine motor skills.
- Some babies first suck on soft foods before they really chew.

How can you support your baby?

- Offer soft, bite-sized pieces that they can grab themselves (e.g. steamed carrots, avocado or banana).
- Allow him to experiment with food - yes, it will be messy, but that's part of it!
- Use non-slip plates or trays to prevent food from slipping away too quickly.

Eating is a sensory experience - it's not just about getting enough to eat, but also about discovering!

7.5 Why your baby needs more closeness now

Some parents are surprised: their baby was previously relaxed, but suddenly clings to them more and hardly wants to be put down.

Why is this happening?

- At six months, a new phase of **strangeness** begins. Your baby now recognises familiar and unfamiliar faces more consciously and prefers to stay close to you.
- It becomes more mobile, but at the same time realises that it is dependent on mum or dad - this can lead to insecurity.
- Emotional developmental leaps are often accompanied by an increased need for closeness.

What you can do:

- Carry your baby more often if he needs it - it gives him security.
- Let it explore its surroundings in a safe environment, but be close by.
- Talk to him calmly if he is a stranger - that way he will feel understood.

This phase is completely normal and will pass with time - your baby simply needs a lot of security now.

Conclusion: A big month full of changes!

The sixth month brings with it huge leaps in development: your baby begins to try solid foods, it becomes more active and perhaps also more affectionate.

What you can take with you:

✓ Complementary feeding is an exciting but individual process - every baby has its own pace.

✓ Breastfeeding or bottle feeding remains important.

✓ Your baby will start to sit up more and explore the world around them.

✓ Eating is a sensory experience - allow your baby to experiment with food.

✓ Closeness and security are particularly important now - your baby needs your security.

The next few months will be even more exciting - soon your baby may be sitting up, crawling and becoming more actively involved in their environment. Enjoy this special phase - it will pass much quicker than you think! 🖤

8 Teething - a challenge for parents and child

Somewhere between the fourth and seventh month, many babies start teething - a process that demands a lot from both parents and child. Some babies get their first teeth almost unnoticed, others struggle with pain, restlessness and poor sleep.

You may notice that your baby is drooling more, putting everything in their mouth or is more restless than usual. These are often the first signs that teething is on its way. But don't worry - with a few helpful tips, you can guide your baby through this phase and give them some relief.

8.1 The first teeth: When and how?

Every baby's teeth are different - some are born with one tooth, others don't have a single tooth at twelve months.

🦷 **When do the first teeth start to appear?**

- Most babies get their first tooth **between** the **fourth and seventh month**.

- The **lower incisors** usually erupt first, followed by the upper incisors.

- By the third birthday, a child normally has a complete set of milk teeth with **20 teeth**.

📌 **Typical tooth eruption:**

✓ **6-10 months:** First incisors at the bottom

✓ **8-12 months:** Upper incisors

✓ **9-16 months:** Lateral incisors

✓ **13-19 months:** First molars

✓ **16-23 months:** Canines

✓ **23-33 months:** Second molars

If your baby has no teeth at six months, this is completely normal - there is no fixed rule for tooth eruption.

8.2 Symptoms of teething - and how you can help

Some babies hardly show any signs of teething, others are fussy for days, sleep badly or even have a slightly elevated temperature.

Typical symptoms of teething:

✓ Increased drooling

✓ Putting everything in the mouth and chewing on it

✓ Red cheeks or sore bottom

✓ Restless sleep or frequent waking up

✓ Reduced appetite

✓ Irritability or clingy behaviour

When should you see a doctor?

- If your baby has a high temperature (over 38.5°C) - teething can cause a slightly higher temperature, but not a high fever.

- If the diarrhoea or restlessness lasts longer than a few days.

- If the gums look extremely swollen or inflamed.

8.3 Teething rings, dental gels and household remedies at a glance

There are many ways to support your baby during teething. Here are some tried and tested methods:

Teething rings - the classic

Teething rings are ideal because they relieve the pressure on the gums and soothe the baby.

✓ **Tip:** Place the teething ring briefly in the fridge (not in the freezer!) so that the cold also helps.

Home remedies for teething pain

- **Cold flannels:** A damp, cooled cloth can be given to bite on.

- **Chilled carrots or cucumber:** If your baby is already eating complementary foods, they can chew on them.

- **Breast milk ice cubes:** Breast milk frozen in a teething ring with a cooling function can help.

Tooth gels and globules - yes or no?

- There are teething gels with soothing active ingredients, but you should speak to your paediatrician beforehand.

- Homeopathic remedies such as Osanit or Chamomilla globules are often recommended, but are scientifically controversial.

Parents as tranquillisers

Sometimes nothing helps better than **closeness and cuddling**. Many babies want to be carried a lot when they are teething - this gives them a sense of security.

8.4 Proper dental care right from the start

As soon as the first tooth appears, dental care begins!

💡 Important:

- From the first tooth onwards, brush once a day with a **soft baby toothbrush** and an **amount of children's toothpaste containing fluoride the size of a grain of rice.**

- Brushing should be done twice a day from the first birthday.

- Do not use honey or sweet teas to soothe your baby - this can lead to tooth decay.

📌 First dental care tips:

✓ Finger toothbrushes or soft baby toothbrushes work well.
✓ Let your baby playfully explore the toothbrush.
✓ Avoid sweet drinks in a bottle - water or unsweetened tea are better.

8.5 Teething and sleep problems: What helps?

Many parents notice that their baby sleeps less well during teething. The pain often seems to be worse at night - this is because the blood flow increases when lying down.

💤 Tips for better sleep when teething:

✓ Gently massage the gums before going to bed.
✓ Offer cooling teething rings or moist cloths to chew on.
✓ Additional closeness and comfort - sometimes just cuddling helps.
✓ Homeopathic or herbal remedies can be tried in consultation with the doctor.

✕ What you should avoid:

- Pain gels with anaesthetics - they can be dangerous if they get into the throat.

- Medication without consulting the paediatrician.

If your baby wakes up often during this time, be patient - this phase will pass. After a few days, when the tooth has erupted, most babies sleep better again.

Conclusion: Teething is a challenge - but it will pass!

Teething is a stressful time for your baby (and for you), but it is part of natural development. Some babies take it in their stride, others struggle more - every child is different.

💡 What you can take with you:

✓ The first teeth usually come in between the 4th and 7th month, but every baby has its own pace.
✓ Typical symptoms are drooling, restlessness and increased chewing.
✓ Teething rings, cooling cloths and lots of closeness can help.
✓ Dental care starts from the first tooth - a good routine prevents problems later on.
✓ Sleeping problems are normal when teething - it usually gets better after a few days.

Even if teething is a real challenge, it's a sign that your baby is growing and developing. And when the first shiny little tooth flashes, all the effort is quickly forgotten! 😍 🦷 🫧

9. the first year - from baby to toddler

A very special event is coming up: your baby will soon be one year old! 🎉 The past twelve months have been an exciting time full of growth, learning and unforgettable moments. Your little miracle has developed from a newborn in need of protection to an active explorer who is curious about his environment.

In this chapter, we take a look at the developmental steps your child has mastered in the first year and what they now find particularly exciting. You will also get tips on how you can support your baby during this exciting phase.

9.1 The first steps: learning to walk

Perhaps your baby is still cautious and is still pulling itself up on furniture, or perhaps it is already taking its first free steps. No matter at what pace your baby learns to walk - it's a big milestone!

👣 **Typical time frame for learning to walk:**
✓ **6-10 months:** Sealing or crawling begins.
✓ **8-12 months:** Your baby pulls himself up on furniture and stands with support.
✓ **10-14 months:** First wobbly steps with support.
✓ **12-18 months:** Free walking - every child walks at their own pace!

🚀 **This way you can help your baby learn to walk:**

- Let your baby **walk barefoot** if possible - this promotes balance.

- A safe play area with a soft floor helps to cushion falls.

- You should secure furniture with sharp edges - your baby will pull itself up everywhere!

- Be patient - some babies walk at 10 months, others only at 15 months. Both are completely normal.

⚠ **Don't stress!** If your baby is not yet sitting up or crawling on its own, give it time. Some babies even skip crawling and go straight to walking.

9.2 First words and language development

Your baby has been practising diligently all year: listening, chatting, babbling - and now they may be saying their first real words!

👣 **How does language develop at this age?**
✓ At 6 months, your baby begins to repeat syllables such as "ba-ba" or "da-da".
✓ At 9 months, they understand their first words such as "no" or "mummy".

✓ At 12 months, they can usually speak 1-3 understandable words (e.g. "mummy", "ball", "woof").

✊ Tips for language promotion:

- Talk to your baby a lot - describe what you are doing ("Now we are cleaning the nappy").

- Repeat simple words ("Look, a cat! Cat!").

- Read to your baby - picture books are great for language development.

- Avoid "baby talk" - a clear "bottle" is better than "baba".

If your child does not yet speak any recognisable words at the age of one, this is not a cause for concern. Language development is very individual - some children only speak their first word at 18 months!

9.3 Why babies put things in their mouths

Have you noticed that your baby puts everything in their mouth? Toys, spoons, your hand, the carpet - simply everything is explored.

💡 Why do babies do this?

✓ They explore the world with all their senses - especially with their mouth!
✓ The mouth is particularly sensitive and helps with feeling.
✓ Teething can trigger an additional urge to chew.

🏠 Safety measures for little explorers:

- Make sure there are no small parts lying around - choking hazard!

- Toys should be free of harmful substances and saliva-proof.

- Check the floor regularly for crumbs or coins - babies grab them in a flash!

Even if it's sometimes annoying when your baby puts a shoe in their mouth again - it's completely normal and part of their development!

9.4 Playing with mum and dad - why it's so important

Your baby loves to play with you! And it's not just a great way to pass the time, it's also important for his mental and social development.

💡 Which games are ideal now?

✓ **Stacking and sorting:** Stacking towers of building blocks or cups promotes fine motor skills.
✓ **Peek-a-boo game:** Your baby begins to understand that things exist even when they are not visible.
✓ **Music and dancing:** Moving to music encourages rhythm and body coordination.
✓ **Rolling and throwing:** A ball is perfect for little hands and helps with learning to move.

Playtime with mum and dad strengthens the bond and gives your baby the security it needs to discover new things.

9.5 The first birthday - a special event

Unbelievable - your baby is one year old! This day is not only an emotional milestone for your child, but also for you as parents.

🎂 **What can the party look like?**

✓ Keep it simple - too many guests or too much hustle and bustle can overwhelm your child.

✓ A small cake or a healthy "baby smash cake" is a great idea.

✓ A few balloons or garlands will make the day extra special.

✓ Games or activities that your baby likes (e.g. ball pool, music games).

🎁 **Gift ideas for the first birthday:**

🎁 Wooden building blocks or pegging games

🎁 Picture books with thick pages

🎁 Cuddly toys or dolls

🎁 Sliding animals or pull-along toys

🎁 A small ride-on car or a baby walker

The first birthday is a wonderful moment to look back on your first year together. You have learnt so much, laughed, maybe even cried - and you have grown as a family.

Conclusion: The first year was an incredible journey!

💡 **What you can take with you:**

✓ Your baby is becoming more mobile - it is crawling or perhaps already taking its first steps.

✓ Speech development is picking up speed - the first understandable words will soon be coming.

✓ Putting everything in your mouth is normal - but make sure it's safe!

✓ Playing with mum and dad is the best form of encouragement.

✓ The first birthday is a special milestone - celebrate it in a relaxed way and with lots of love.

The first year is full of magical moments. Enjoy the time - your baby will never be as small again. 🖤 🎉

10. the defiant phase begins - autonomy and tantrums

Congratulations! Your child is no longer a baby, but a toddler. The first birthday marks the beginning of an exciting but also challenging phase: the so-called "defiant phase" or, to be more precise, the phase of **developing autonomy**.

You may have noticed that your child says "No!" more often, resists getting dressed with all their might or suddenly throws a tantrum when they don't get what they want. Welcome to one of the most important phases of your child's development!

In this chapter, you will learn why this phase is so important, how you can lovingly accompany tantrums and why boundaries are just as important as freedom.

10.1 Why children suddenly say "No!"

One minute your child was sweet and uncomplicated - and the next they just seem to be saying "No!". Whether it's about eating, getting dressed or brushing their teeth, your child protests against everything. But why?

What is behind the "defiant phase"?

- Your child discovers its own will and wants to decide for itself.

- It understands that it is an independent person who can influence things.

- It tests limits: How far can I go? What happens if I say no?

- It often has strong emotions, but is not yet able to control them well.

What can you do?

- **Be patient:** Your child is not being defiant to annoy you - they are learning to regulate their feelings.

- **Offer alternatives:** Instead of "Put your jacket!" rather "Would you like to wear the blue or the red jacket?"

- **Stay calm:** If you get upset, the situation often escalates even more.

📌 **Important:** A "No!" doesn't mean that your child doesn't listen - it shows that they are developing their own opinion. This is a good sign of healthy emotional development!

10.2 Understanding and accompanying outbursts of anger

Sudden screaming, throwing themselves on the floor, desperate tears - tantrums can be violent, and as a parent it can be hard to deal with.

Why do children throw tantrums?

- They are frustrated because they don't get something or don't manage something.

- They cannot yet control their emotions - their brains are not yet mature enough for this.

- You feel overwhelmed or tired.

- They want independence, but at the same time are still dependent on help.

How can you support your child during a tantrum?

✓ **Stay calm** - your child can sense your emotions. If you stay calm, they can calm down more quickly.

✓ **Show understanding:** "I can see that you're very angry right now. That's okay."

✓ **Set clear but loving boundaries:** "I understand that you don't like this, but we can't run into the street."

✓ **Let your child express their feelings:** Sometimes it helps to just be there until your child calms down.

✓ **Comfort them after the tantrum:** As soon as your child has calmed down, they need you to be close and safe.

🔔 **What you should avoid:**

❌ Don't shout or punish - this only increases the anger.

❌ Don't give in immediately - if your child always gets what they want, they won't learn how to deal with frustration.

📌 **Important:** Tantrums are part of development. Your child will learn how to deal with frustration - a skill they will need for the rest of their lives!

10.3 Staying patient - tips for stressful moments

There are days when your child seems to be defiant for no reason. Maybe you're tired, stressed or just don't have the energy for another tantrum.

How can you stay calm in these moments?

✓ **Take a deep breath** - Three deep breaths help you to collect yourself.

✓ **Count to ten internally** - This helps you not to react impulsively.

✓ **Remember: It's just a phase!** - Even if it's exhausting now, it will get better.

✓ **Take a short break if necessary** - If you realise that you are getting angry, step out of the situation briefly.

💡 **Tip:** If your child is having a tantrum, imagine they are a small adult who is struggling with strong emotions. How would you talk to them? This perspective can help you stay calm.

10.4 Loving consistency: setting boundaries

Children not only need freedom, but also clear rules and boundaries. Without rules, children feel insecure - they need a structure that they can orientate themselves by.

How do you set loving boundaries?

✓ **Remain consistent:** If you say "no" once, then stick to it.

✓ **Be understanding:** Explain why a rule applies ("We stop on the road because cars are dangerous").

✓ **Avoid too many rules at once:** only set rules that are really important.

✓ **Stay calm and friendly**: "I understand that you want it, but I can't do it now."

📌 **Important:** Boundaries are not there to annoy your child - they give them security.

10.5 The importance of choice

💡 **Small decisions give your child a sense of control.**

Instead of giving your child a fixed decision ("Put your shoes on!"), you can involve them in the process:

✓ "Do you want to put on the red shoes or the blue shoes?"

✓ "Do you want to brush your teeth first or put on your pyjamas first?"

✓ "Do you prefer apple or banana?"

Why does it work?

- Your child feels taken seriously.
- It can express its will without being defiant.
- It gains self-confidence in its decisions.

⚠ **But be careful:** too many decisions can overwhelm your child. Choose a maximum of two alternatives!

Conclusion: The defiant phase is an important learning time for your child

The autonomy phase is exhausting, but it is also an incredibly valuable time for your child. They learn to discover their own will, test boundaries and deal with frustration.

What you can take away:

✓ A "No!" is a sign of development - your child is discovering their own will.

✓ Tantrums are normal and need loving support, not punishment.

✓ Patience and calmness will help you to deal with stressful moments.

✓ Boundaries give your child security - but they should be clear and understandable.

✓ Small decisions make your child more independent and reduce defiant behaviour.

Even if this phase is sometimes exhausting, it is a sign that your child is growing, learning and developing their own personality. And in the end, that's exactly what we want as parents, isn't it?

---

11 The second year of life - motor skills and movement

When your child turns two, they become increasingly active and mobile. They may have just taken their first steps or are already scampering safely around the house. The world now becomes a huge adventure playground for your toddler, which they explore with enthusiasm.

During this phase, your child not only develops their gross motor skills (walking, climbing, running), but also their fine motor skills (grasping, sorting things, turning pages). At the same time, their self-confidence grows - they want to do more and more things **on their own**.

How can you support your child during this exciting phase? Which forms of movement are particularly important now? And how do you deal with the first falls and minor accidents?

11.1 Climbing, running, jumping - the child in motion

You may have noticed that your child is hardly sitting still now. Where it was still cautious before, it is now daring more and more. They walk more confidently, start to run, climb onto the sofa or try their first little jumps.

Typical motor development steps in the second year of life:
✓ 12-15 months: Safe walking, first attempts to run
✓ 16-18 months: Climbing stairs with holding on, climbing on furniture
✓ 18-24 months: hopping, walking backwards, kicking a ball

This development is important because movement strengthens your child's muscles, trains their balance and teaches them to judge themselves better.

How can you support your child?

- Encourage them to **move freely** - without fear, but with safety precautions.

- Let it run in nature, climb on playgrounds and jump on soft ground.

- Play movement games such as "catch me" or "hop like a rabbit".

- Build small **obstacle courses** in the home with cushions and mattresses.

Tip: Instead of constantly shouting "Careful!", actively accompany your child and help them to recognise their limits.

11.2 Why accidents are happening more frequently now

As curiosity and agility grow, so does the risk of accidents. Your child doesn't yet understand what dangers there are - they see the world as one big playground.

Typical accidents at this age:

- Stumbling and falling when learning to walk

- Falls from the sofa or chairs

- Headbutting on furniture

- Fingers trapped in doors or drawers

- Putting small objects in the mouth

How can you childproof your home?

✓ Fit **corner and edge protectors** to sharp furniture edges.
✓ Fit **stair gates** if there are stairs in the house.
✓ **Secure sockets** with child safety locks.
✓ **Secure furniture** that could tip over (shelves, chests of drawers).
✓ **Secure danger areas**, e.g. keep a close eye on the kitchen or balcony.

Important: Falls are part of development. Your child will learn to control their movements better. You should only take a closer look if they keep falling or injure themselves frequently.

11.3 Safety measures for the home

Children are incredibly quick! One moment of inattention and your child is on the coffee table or climbing onto a chair.

These safety measures will help:

✓ Keep **cleaning products and medicines** out of reach.

✓ Avoid **loose tablecloths** that can be pulled down.

✓ Keep hot drinks out of your child's reach.

✓ **Don't leave your child unattended in the bath!**

⚠ **Important:** Despite all caution - your child should still be allowed to explore their surroundings. Excessive prohibitions can lead to anxiety.

11.4 The first wheel and tricycle attempts

Many children are now interested in balance bikes or tricycles. These vehicles are a great way to train balance and coordination.

When is the right time for a balance bike?

- Usually **between 18 and 24 months**, when your child can walk safely.

- It should be able to put its feet firmly on the ground to push itself off.

- It should have enough balance to avoid constantly tipping over.

Advantages of the balance bike:

✓ Promotes balance and makes it easier to switch to a bike later on.

✓ Strengthens leg muscles and coordination.

✓ Gives the child a feeling of independence and speed.

Tip: Start with a model with a low seat height and make sure your child is wearing a helmet.

11.5 Promoting fine motor skills in everyday life

In addition to gross motor skills, your child's fine motor skills are now also developing. They can work with their fingers more and more purposefully - this is an important preparation for later skills such as painting, writing and eating independently.

What can your child already do at this age?

✓ Eat with a spoon (even if it still spills)

✓ Build towers with building blocks

✓ Pressing small buttons or grasping toys

✓ Turning pages in a book

How can you promote fine motor skills through play?

✓ **Let your child eat with their hands** - this trains their tweezer grip (thumb-index finger grip).

✓ **Give them simple tasks** such as "Put the pasta in the bottle" or "Sort the colours".

✓ **Paint with finger paints** or let them experiment with modelling clay.

✓ Offer **pegging games or puzzles** with large pieces.

📌 **Tip:** Be patient - your child learns through repetition. It doesn't have to be "perfect", it has to be fun!

Conclusion: Your child is becoming more and more independent!

The second year of life is an exciting time: your child becomes more confident in their movements, discovers their surroundings with new enthusiasm and wants to do many things themselves.

🏆 **What you can take with you:**

✓ Your child needs **exercise** - encourage them to run, climb and jump.

✓ Small **falls are normal** - they help your child to recognise their limits.

✓ A **safe home** gives your child the opportunity to move freely.

✓ **Balance bikes and tricycles** are great first vehicles for developing coordination.

✓ **Fine motor skills are developing** - simple games with the hands are ideal.

Even if your child is now becoming more active and independent, they will always come back to you for security and closeness. Be there, support them, but also give them their space. This is the best way for your child to learn to go out into the world with confidence! 🚀 💕

12. language development - how children learn to speak

Language is one of the most fascinating tools that your child learns in the course of their development. From the first babble to the first words to small conversations - language development in the second year of life is rapid and full of surprises.

Perhaps your child has already said "mummy" or "daddy" or is starting to use individual words. They already understand much more than they can say themselves and are picking up new words every day. But how exactly does language develop? What can you do to encourage your child through play? And when should you pay attention if your child is not yet speaking?

In this chapter, you will learn all about your child's exciting language development.

12.1 From one-word sentences to small conversations

In the first few months, your baby was above all a good listener. It recognised your voice and reacted to your words. But now it is actively going one step further: it is starting to form its own words and speak its first small sentences.

🏆 **Typical language development:**

✓ **6-12 months:** First syllables ("Ba-Ba", "Da-Da")

✓ **12-18 months:** One-word sentences ("ball", "car", "woof")

✓ **18-24 months:** Two-word combinations ("Mummy come", "more banana")

✓ **24-30 months:** First small sentences with three to four words ("I want that").

What happens linguistically in the second year of life?

- Your child already understands **much more** than he or she can speak.

- It combines familiar words with their meaning ("car" = vehicle outside).

- It begins to use words for wishes or observations.

- The first two-word combinations are created.

📌 **Important:** Every child develops differently! Some children already speak many words at 18 months, others take until their third birthday.

12.2 Why your child likes to parrot

Have you noticed that your child often imitates words or sounds? Babbling is an important part of language development.

💡 **Why do children imitate speech?**

✓ Language is a social tool - your child wants to communicate with you.
✓ They learn by imitation - the more they hear, the more they memorise.
✓ They want to communicate with you and try out new sounds.

This is how you can support your child:

- Speak to him slowly and clearly.

- Repeat simple terms: "Yes, that's a ball. A red ball."

- Avoid "baby talk" - use clear, simple words.

- Praise your child for their attempts at speaking: "Yes, you said that really well!"

📌 **Important:** Your child doesn't have to speak perfectly - it learns through trial and error. Be patient!

12.3 Books and songs for language development

One of the best ways to promote language development is to read aloud and sing together.

📖 **Why are books so important?**

✓ They expand your child's vocabulary.
✓ Your child learns new terms in context.
✓ It encourages attention and listening skills.
✓ Reading aloud together strengthens the bond between you.

🎶 **Why do songs help?**

✓ Children love repetition - songs are easy to remember.
✓ Rhymes and melodies support the feeling for language.
✓ Your child learns new words through play.

Tip: Which books are suitable?

- **Cardboard picture books** with clear pictures and few words.

- **Rhymes and finger plays** ("Bake, bake cake").

- **Sound books** that imitate sounds.

📌 **Tip:** Your child doesn't have to understand all the words - the important thing is spending time with you!

12.4 Recognising and acting on language delays

Every child learns to speak at their own pace. While some children already speak many words by the age of two, others only use a few.

🔔 **When should you start paying attention?**

🚩 At 18 months: Your child **does not yet** speak any words.

🚩 At 24 months: Your child speaks **fewer than 20 words**.

🚩 At 30 months: Your child **does not speak two-word sentences** ("Daddy come").

🚩 Your child shows **no interest in language** (no gestures, no attempts to speak).

📌 **What to do if your child doesn't speak much?**

- Talk to your child a lot - describe what you are doing ("I'm cutting a banana").

- Use picture books and repeat terms.

- Avoid pressure - language develops playfully.

- Observe your child - if you are worried, talk to your paediatrician.

📌 **Important:** Some children are "silent observers" - they listen for a long time and only speak later.

12.5 Multilingualism - curse or blessing?

Many parents wonder whether their child is confused when they hear several languages. But the opposite is true! Multilingualism is a gift that will accompany your child throughout their life.

🔔 **How do children learn several languages?**

✓ Babies are prepared for multilingualism from birth.

✓ They can easily separate different languages.

✓ Children need regular contact with each language in order to use it actively.

Tips for multilingual education:

- Choose a clear strategy: **One person - one language** (e.g. mum speaks German, dad speaks English).

- Use everyday situations: Speak in the respective language when eating, playing or going for a walk.

- Offer songs, books and games in different languages.

- Be patient - sometimes children mix words from different languages (this is normal!).

📌 **Important:** Multilingualism does NOT delay language development! Multilingual children often start speaking later, but catch up quickly.

Conclusion: Accompanying your child on the path to language

Language development is an exciting process that is characterised by many small steps. Some children speak early, others take their time - both are normal.

💡 **What you can take with you:**
✓ Your child understands much more than they can say - be patient!
✓ Repetition helps - talk to your child a lot and use books and songs.
✓ Imitation is key - your child learns by listening.
✓ Language delays are rarely a cause for concern - but watch your child.
✓ Multilingualism is an advantage - use it if you speak several languages!

The best thing about language development? The moment when your child says "I love you" for the first time. 😊 🤍

13. getting clean - a big step towards independence

Potty training is an important developmental step for your child - and a big issue for many parents. While some children seem to learn to use the potty on their own, others take much longer and don't want to sit on it at all.

You may be asking yourself: **When is the right time? How can I support my child? And how can I avoid stress when getting clean?**

The good news is that every child will eventually become dry. The process is individual and can take different lengths of time between the ages of two and four. It is important that you remain patient and lovingly accompany your child.

13.1 When is the right time?

Not every child is ready for potty training at the same age. While some show interest as early as 18 months, others are not ready until they are three or four years old.

💡 **Signs that your child is ready:**
✓ They can control their bladder and bowels better (e.g. their nappy stays dry for longer).
✓ They show interest in the potty or toilet ("Mummy, what are you doing?").
✓ He can understand simple instructions ("Sit on the potty").
✓ Tells you when the nappy is wet or dirty.
✓ He no longer likes the nappy and wants to be "like the grown-ups".

📌 **Important:** There is no right age - your child sets the pace!

13.2 Potty training without stress

The most important thing when getting clean is a relaxed posture. The less pressure, the easier it is.

🚽 How can you gently get your child used to the potty?

- Place **a potty or toilet seat** within sight (e.g. in the bathroom).

- Let your child **sit on it with clothes on** to get used to it.

- Playfully explain what the potty is for.

- **Imitation helps** - if your child sees mum or dad going to the toilet, they will understand the context more quickly.

- Praise your child when they show interest - but don't put any pressure on them!

📌 **Tip:** Read books about the potty to your child (e.g. "Conni goes to the potty").

13.3 Night nappies - when to do without them?

Getting dry during the day is the first step - at night it is often more difficult. Some children still need a nappy at night for a long time because they cannot control their bladder during sleep.

💡 When is your child ready for the night without a nappy?
✓ The nappy is dry in the morning for several days in a row.
✓ Your child wakes up at night and says they need to go to the toilet.
✓ They can go to the toilet reliably during the day.

Tips for drier nights:

✓ Let your child go to the toilet again in the evening.
✓ Protect the mattress with a waterproof protective cover.
✓ Don't wake your child at night - it often doesn't help.

📌 **Important:** It is completely normal for children to wet the bed occasionally up to the age of five!

13.4 Mastering adversity calmly

There will always be accidents - that's part of the learning process!

💡 What to do if something goes wrong?

- **Stay calm!** No child wets their pants on purpose.

- **No scolding!** Negative reactions can cause anxiety.

- **Encourage your child:** "It can happen. It will definitely work next time."

- **Always have spare clothes with you** when you are travelling.

Tip: Sometimes relapses are normal, e.g. due to stress or changes (starting kindergarten, having a sibling). Be patient!

13.5 Reward systems: yes or no?

Many parents consider rewarding their child for going potty - for example with stickers or small surprises.

Pro reward system:
✓ Can be an additional motivation for some children.
✓ Gives positive reinforcement for small successes.
✓ Makes the whole thing more playful.

Contra reward system:
✗ Can build up pressure ("I have to go to the potty to get something").
✗ Can lead to the child later only going to the toilet with a reward.

Alternative: Instead of material rewards, use praise and encouragement: "Great job, I'm proud of you!"

Conclusion: Your child sets the pace!

Getting clean is a natural process that takes time. Some children are dry at the age of two, others at four - and that's perfectly okay!

What you can take with you:
✓ Don't stress - every child gets dry eventually.
✓ Look out for signs that your child is ready.
✓ Potty training should be playful and without pressure.
✓ Night nappies are often necessary for longer - patience helps.
✓ Mishaps are normal and are part of the learning process.

With a relaxed attitude and loving guidance, your child will master getting clean - at their own pace! 🚽 💜

14. entering the daycare centre - a new world

Starting daycare is a big milestone - both for your child and for you as a parent. Suddenly your child is no longer with you around the clock, but spends time with new people, gets to know other children and discovers a completely new environment.

While some children start kindergarten full of joy, others need more time to get used to the new situation. You may be wondering: **How will my child fit in? Will it cry when I leave? What can I do to make the transition smoother?**

In this chapter, you will find out how to find the right daycare centre, what settling-in methods are available and how to prepare your child (and yourself) for this big step.

14.1 Finding the right daycare centre

Not every daycare centre is suitable for every child - so it's worth looking for the right facility early on.

💡 **What should you look out for when choosing a daycare centre?**

✓ **Educational concept**: Is it a traditional daycare centre, a Montessori or Waldorf facility?

✓ **Childcare times:** Are the times compatible with your everyday life?

✓ **Group size and childcare ratio**: How many children are there for every specialist?

✓ **Familiarisation concept**: Is emphasis placed on a gentle familiarisation process?

✓ **Atmosphere**: Does the daycare centre feel warm and inviting?

👉 **Tip:** Visit the daycare centre together with your child and observe how they react to the environment.

14.2 Gentle familiarisation

The first step in daycare is the **familiarisation phase**. It helps your child to slowly get used to the new environment, the teachers and the other children.

What familiarisation methods are there?

1️⃣ Berlin model (most common method):

- **Day 1-3:** You stay at the daycare centre with your child and they explore the surroundings.

- **Day 4:** First short separation attempt (10-15 minutes).

- **Day 5-10:** The separation time is slowly extended depending on your child's reaction.

2️⃣ Munich model:

- Slower acclimatisation in which the child's needs are taken into account.

- The child determines the pace of separation.

👉 **Important:** A good familiarisation process takes 2-6 weeks, depending on the child.

14.3 Overcoming separation anxiety

Many children cry at first when they are told to stay at the daycare centre - and that is completely normal! They first have to learn that although you are leaving, you will always come back.

How can you alleviate separation anxiety?

✓ **Short, affectionate goodbyes:** Avoid prolonged hesitation or going back.

✓ **Create rituals:** A kiss goodbye, a hug or a little "goodbye ritual" will help your child.

✓ **Show confidence:** If you appear confident, your child will sense that everything is okay.

✓ **Give a cuddly toy or scarf:** A familiar object can provide comfort.

Tip: You will also feel the separation - that's completely normal! Stay positive and trust that your child will find their place in the daycare centre.

14.4 Making first friends

At daycare, your child will interact regularly with other children for the first time. However, friendships develop slowly - many children still play alongside each other at this age (parallel play).

What happens in this phase?

✓ First interest in other children ("That's my friend!").

✓ First social conflicts (taking toys away, fighting over places).

✓ Development of empathy - the child learns to empathise with others.

How can you promote social skills?

- Play role-playing games with your child ("What to do when someone is sad?").

- Encourage joint activities with other children (playground visits).

- Talk about feelings: "How does your friend feel when you take the toy away from him?"

14.5 Strengthening daycare centre diseases and the immune system

"Ever since my child started going to daycare, he's been sick all the time!" - Many parents know this phrase. In fact, your child encounters numerous new germs at daycare that challenge their immune system.

Typical daycare centre illnesses:

✓ Colds (cough, runny nose, fever)

✓ Gastrointestinal infections

✓ Hand, foot and mouth disease

✓ conjunctivitis

How can you strengthen your child's immune system?

✓ Lots of fresh air and outdoor exercise.

✓ A balanced diet with plenty of fruit and vegetables.

✓ Sufficient sleep and relaxation.

✓ Wash your hands regularly.

⚠ **Important:** A strong immune system only develops over time. It is normal for your child to get sick often at daycare - but they will be more robust later at school!

Conclusion: Starting daycare is a big change - for everyone!

Starting daycare is a big step towards independence. Your child gets to know new people, has their first social experiences and discovers a new world full of adventures.

What you can take with you:
✔ Choosing a daycare centre carefully is important - your child should feel comfortable.
✔ Settling in takes time - be patient.
✔ Separation anxiety is normal - loving rituals help.
✔ First friendships develop slowly - support your child in this process.
✔ Daycare centre illnesses are part of it - the immune system has to learn first.

Even though starting daycare can be challenging, your child will soon come home with shining eyes and be excited to tell you all about their experiences!

15. sibling love - from only child to big brother or big sister

The arrival of a new sibling is a significant event for the whole family - especially for the older child. While parents are happy about the new addition to the family, the first-born child often experiences the situation differently: suddenly they have to share mum and dad, receive less attention and are confronted with a completely new family structure.

This change can trigger many emotions - from curiosity and pride to jealousy and insecurity. But don't worry: with the right preparation and lots of love, you can help your child to settle into their new role as big brother or big sister.

15.1 How to prepare your child for a sibling

The earlier you prepare your child for the new baby, the better they will be able to adjust to the changes.

Tips for preparation:
✔ **Explain what is happening in an age-appropriate way:** "Soon you'll have a baby brother or sister. It's growing in mum's tummy right now."
✔ **Involve your child:** Let them stroke the baby bump or look at ultrasound pictures.
✔ **Tell stories about siblings:** Books help to make the concept easier to understand.
✔ **Change routines early on**: If your child will soon have a new room or be carried less, get them used to it slowly.
✔ **Make the big sibling proud**: "You're going to be a big brother / sister - that's something very special!"

👉 **Tip:** Make sure that your child doesn't get the feeling that the baby is "more important". It still needs lots of attention and love.

15.2 Understanding and accompanying jealousy

It is quite normal for an older child to be jealous of the baby - after all, they now have to share their parents. Some children react with withdrawal, others with anger or suddenly demand more attention again.

How does jealousy manifest itself?

- Your child will become more affectionate and demand more cuddles.

- It behaves like a baby again (wants to be carried, talks like a toddler).

- It annoys or ignores the baby.

- It seeks attention - sometimes with tantrums.

What helps with jealousy?

✓ **Give your child exclusive time:** Plan deliberate moments only with the older sibling.
✓ **Praise positive behaviour**: "You played so nicely with the baby - that makes me very happy!"
✓ **Actively involve them:** "Can you help me change the baby?"
✓ **Show understanding for their feelings:** "I understand that you are sometimes sad because mummy has to look after the baby."

📌 **Important:** Your child is allowed to be annoyed or angry with the baby sometimes - that's normal! Help them to deal with these feelings without punishing them.

15.3 Time for every child: the balancing act

One of the biggest challenges for parents with several children is to do justice to each child. The older child should not feel neglected, while the baby naturally needs a lot of attention.

💡 **Tips for a good balance:**
✓ **Schedule exclusive time for the older child** - even if it's only 10 minutes a day.
✓ **Let your child take on "big sibling" tasks** (e.g. fetching a nappy or helping with dressing).
✓ **Avoid comparisons:** "Your brother can already do that, why can't you?" - This can lead to frustration.
✓ **Pay attention to your choice of words:** Instead of "I can't because the baby is hungry", use "I'll get the baby ready for a minute, then we'll play."

📌 **Tip:** If you praise your child, don't do it at the baby's expense ("You're much better behaved than your brother"), but independently.

15.4 Learning about sibling conflict and reconciliation

Disputes between siblings are unavoidable - but they are also an important part of social development. Your child learns to resolve conflicts, negotiate and assert themselves.

💡 **Typical topics of dispute between siblings:**
✓ Toys ("That's mine!")
✓ Attention from parents ("Mum, you're just looking after the baby!")
✓ Physical contact (e.g. the baby pulls the big sibling's hair).

How can you deal with sibling disputes?

✓ **Stay calm and objective** - don't shout or take sides.
✓ **Help your child to express their feelings:** "I can see that you're angry because your brother your toy."

✓ **Be supportive, but don't resolve the argument immediately:** "How can you solve the problem?"

✓ **Mediate if necessary**: "You can play with the car and then give it to your sister."

✓ **Don't make constant comparisons** ("But your sister is much nicer than you!").

✦ **Tip:** Siblings learn how to assert themselves through arguments - as long as it doesn't become unfair or hurtful, they are allowed to argue.

15.5 Shared rituals for sibling bonding

Even if there are sometimes conflicts, siblings can become a wonderful team. Shared rituals help to strengthen the bond between the children.

Beautiful rituals for siblings:

✓ **Reading bedtime stories together** - this strengthens the bond.

✓ **"Just the two of us" days** - special outings with just mum or dad.

✓ **Daily hug or greeting ritual** - for example, a high-five or a little song.

✓ **Games where they have to work together** - e.g. puzzles or building blocks.

✓ **Read stories about siblings** - this helps them to better accept the role of "big brother" or "big sister".

✦ **Tip:** No child should feel obliged to love the baby all the time - but shared rituals can promote bonding.

Conclusion: Sibling love grows with time

Having a new sibling is a big change for the older child. Jealousy, arguments and frustration are completely normal - but with patience and loving support, a close sibling bond can develop.

💡 **What you can take with you:**

✓ Prepare your child for the baby early on.

✓ Jealousy is normal - continue to give your child lots of attention.

✓ Avoid comparisons and create exclusive time for each child.

✓ Arguing is an important learning process - mediate, but don't solve everything for them.

✓ Shared rituals help to strengthen the sibling bond.

Even if the start is sometimes bumpy, over time your children will not only become siblings, but perhaps best friends for life. 🖤 👶 👶

16 The third year - Seeing the world with new eyes

The third birthday marks the start of an exciting phase in your child's development. They become increasingly independent, ask countless questions and want to discover the world with their own eyes. The famous phrase **"Why?"** becomes a constant companion, as your child now develops a deep interest in understanding connections.

At this age, children often show a mixture of curiosity, creativity and sometimes defiance. They want to do things on their own, but at the same time still need the security of their parents. Emotions play a major role and children at this age often experience intense emotional swings.

How can you support your child in this phase? What developmental steps lie ahead? And how do you best deal with the endless flood of "why" questions?

16.1 Why your child is suddenly questioning everything

The "why questions" phase is a sign of your child's cognitive development. They are beginning to understand that the world works according to certain rules and want to find out what these rules are.

Why does your child ask so many questions?
✓ They want to understand cause and effect ("Why is it raining?").
✓ They are interested in connections ("Why do I have to sleep?").
✓ They discover new concepts ("Why is the sky blue?").
✓ They test how far they can go with questions ("Why can't I do that?").

How can you respond to the "why" questions?

✓ **Take the questions seriously:** Your child is not asking out of boredom, but because they are genuinely curious.
✓ **Explain in a child-friendly way:** simple answers are often enough ("The sky is blue because the sunlight is refracted in the air.').
✓ **Pass on your knowledge, but don't overwhelm:** "That's an exciting question! Let's have a look together."
✓ **Sometimes a counter-question is exciting:** "Why do you think the cat is meowing?"

📌 **Tip:** If the flood of questions overwhelms you, stay calm. Your child is aware of your interest - and that's what counts.

16.2 Encouraging imagination and role play

At this age, your child's imagination becomes more and more developed. Suddenly a cardboard box becomes a spaceship, a stick becomes a magic wand and the sofa becomes a knight's castle.

Why is imagination important?
✓ It helps to understand and re-enact the world.
✓ It promotes creativity and problem-solving skills.
✓ It makes it possible to express feelings.

This way you can support your child's imagination:

✓ **Let your child play freely** - without too many guidelines.
✓ **Offer materials for role play:** Dress-up clothes, cuddly toys, dolls or building blocks.

✓ **Play actively:** Join in without dictating where the game goes.

✓ **Read out imaginative stories** and let your child continue the story.

📌 **Tip:** Role play is not only fun, but also important for your child's social and emotional development.

16.3 The first fears - monsters under the bed?

Many children start to develop fears at the age of three. Suddenly your child is afraid of dark rooms, ghosts or loud noises.

🕯 **Typical fears at this age:**

✓ Darkness or shadows

✓ Separation from parents

✓ Loud noises (e.g. thunderstorms or hoovers)

✓ Monsters or ghosts

How can you help your child?

✓ **Take the fear seriously:** Don't say "That's rubbish", but "I understand that you're scared."

✓ **Offer reassurance**: "I'm here, you're safe."

✓ **Let your child overcome their fears through play:** Draw the monster and "chase" it away together.

✓ **Use routines:** A night light or a bedtime story can help to reduce the fear of the dark.

📌 **Important:** Fears are a sign of a growing imagination - this is completely normal!

16.4 Strengthening emotional intelligence

Three-year-old children often have strong emotions - ranging from being sky-high to outbursts of anger in a matter of seconds. The challenge is that they are not yet able to control these emotions properly.

🕯 **How can you support your child emotionally?**

✓ **Help them to name their feelings:** "Are you sad because your tower has fallen down?"

✓ **Show that all emotions are allowed:** "It's okay to be angry. But we don't hit anyone."

✓ **Offer a way to process emotions:** Colouring, kneading or cuddling often help.

✓ **Show role models:** Your child learns how you deal with feelings by imitation.

📌 **Tip:** Patience is key - your child is just learning to deal with big emotions.

16.5 Why "I can do it alone!" is so important

The urge to be independent comes at the age of three. Your child wants to do things on their own - even if it takes longer or goes wrong.

Why is independence so important?

✓ It strengthens self-confidence.
✓ It gives your child a sense of control.
✓ It helps to develop frustration tolerance.

How can you encourage your child?

✓ **Let them try things out for themselves:** Even if the shirt is the wrong way round - that's okay!
✓ **Give clear, simple instructions:** "You can put the shoes on, I'll help you with the laces."
✓ **Praise the process, not just the result**: "You tried, that's great!"
✓ **Avoid intervening too quickly:** If your child can help themselves, this promotes their independence.

✦ **Tip:** Patience is required - it may take your child 10 minutes to put on their jacket. But this exercise is important!

Conclusion: Your child will become more and more curious and independent!

The third year of life is a time full of questions, emotions and imagination. Your child discovers the world in new ways and learns to become more and more independent.

What you can take with you:

✓ The "why" phase is a sign of cognitive development - stay patient.
✓ Role play and fantasy worlds are important for your child's creativity.
✓ Fears are normal - take them seriously and offer reassurance.
✓ Emotions can be strong - help your child to name them.
✓ The desire for independence is important - let your child try things out.

Even if it is sometimes exhausting - this phase is incredibly valuable. Your child develops their own personality, learns to understand the world and discovers that they can influence many things themselves. Enjoy this exciting time! 🖤 ✦

---

17. dealing with feelings - anger, sadness, joy

The third year of life is an emotional rollercoaster: your child experiences joy, anger, sadness, pride, frustration - and often all in one day. Whereas in the first two years of life, your child mainly reacted to immediate needs (hunger, tiredness, closeness), they are now beginning to recognise feelings more consciously.

However, although your child feels emotions, they are not yet able to name or control them properly. This can lead to outbursts of anger, sudden crying or intense expressions of joy. Your job as a parent is to guide your child through this emotional development and help them to deal with their feelings.

How can you support your child? How can you accompany strong emotions without suppressing them? And how can you help your child to develop empathy for others?

17.1 Why toddlers are often frustrated

Frustration is part of development - especially in the third year of life. Your child wants to do many things themselves, but often comes up against limits.

   Why does your child get frustrated so quickly?

✓ They can't yet do everything the way they want to (e.g. tying shoes, solving puzzles).

✓ They have a strong will, but not always the skills to realise it.

✓ They are not yet able to regulate their emotions - small setbacks feel like major crises for your child.

✓ They don't yet understand that some things take time.

   Example: Your child wants to zip up their jacket on their own, but it doesn't work. He throws the jacket on the floor in frustration and screams.

How can you help?

✓ **Show understanding:** "This is really difficult, isn't it? Let me help you a little."

✓ **Give a little help, but don't solve everything:** let your child keep trying.

✓ **Stay calm:** Your child mirrors your reaction - the calmer you stay, the quicker they will calm down.

   Tip: Frustration tolerance is an important skill - the more your child practises dealing with setbacks, the better they will be at overcoming challenges later on.

17.2 How parents comfort properly

Sometimes your child cries for seemingly trivial reasons - because a banana has broken in half or because they have been given the wrong plate. For us adults, these are small things, but for your child they can trigger big emotions.

   Why is your child crying so intensely?

✓ His brain still processes emotions differently - they come out unfiltered.

✓ They cannot yet put their feelings into words.

✓ They feel pain or disappointment much more directly than adults.

How can you comfort your child?

✓ **Take their feelings seriously:** "I can see that you're sad because your tower has fallen over."

✓ **Offer physical contact:** Some children need a hug or just closeness.

✓ **Avoid distraction or trivialisation:** "Oh, that's not so bad!" signals that his feelings are not important.

✓ **Name the emotion:** "You're angry right now because you wanted to play."

   Important: Your child does not have to stop crying immediately - they should learn that all feelings are allowed.

17.3 Learning to express and share joy

Joy is one of the most beautiful emotions - and your child will learn to show and share it more and more consciously.

How does your child show joy?

✓ They laugh loudly and infectiously.

✓ They jump up and down, clap or hug you.

✓ They talk enthusiastically about experiences ("Mummy, look!").

How can you support this joy?

✓ **Celebrate your child's successes with them!** "Wow, you did the puzzle on your own!"

✓ **Learn to be happy about little things - children see the magic in everyday life.**

✓ **Share your own joy with your child - they learn by imitation.**

✓ **Help your child to share joy with others:** "Would you like to tell Grandma about your great picture?"

📌 **Tip:** Joy grows when you share it - encourage your child to do so!

17.4 Accompanying tantrums without punishing

Anger is one of the most challenging emotions for parents. A tantrum can be loud, intense and unpredictable - but it is an important way for your child to deal with frustration.

Why do children have tantrums?

✓ They are overwhelmed by a situation (e.g. because they are not getting what they want).

✓ They have strong emotions but cannot yet control them.

✓ They are tired, hungry or overstimulated.

How can you react to a tantrum?

✓ **Stay calm:** Even if your child cries - keep your composure.

✓ **Tell him that his feelings are okay:** "I can see you're angry."

✓ **Offer reassurance:** Some children want to be hugged, others need space.

✓ **Avoid punishments or reprimands:** "If you don't stop, you're going to the room!" signals that anger is not allowed.

📌 **Tip:** A tantrum is not manipulation - your child simply can't express their emotions in any other way yet.

17.5 The importance of routines for emotional security

Children need structure to feel safe - especially when it comes to strong emotions.

Why do routines help?

✓ They provide security: the child knows what will happen next.

✓ They reduce stress: fewer surprises = less frustration.

✓ They help to regulate emotions: Clear routines make it easier to deal with feelings.

Examples of helpful routines:

✔ **Morning ritual:** Always get up, get dressed and have breakfast in the same order.

✔ **Bedtime ritual:** Read a book, dim the lights, play soft music or a cuddly toy to calm you down.

✔ **Create "islands of calm":** A place where your child can calm down when things get too much.

📌 **Tip:** Your child needs to feel that their emotions are being seen - but it helps if they know what's coming next.

Conclusion: Emotions are an important part of development

In the third year of life, your child learns to deal with emotions - a process that takes time and support.

 What you can take away:

✔ Frustration is normal - it helps your child to overcome challenges.

✔ Comfort your child without minimising their feelings.

✔ Joy is greater when it is shared - celebrate your child's successes!

✔ Tantrums are not bad behaviour - they are an expression of strong feelings.

✔ Routines help your child to feel safe and deal with emotions.

Even if it is sometimes exhausting - your child is making huge progress in their emotional development. With your loving support, they will learn to understand and manage their feelings. 🩶

18. nutrition in infancy - developing healthy eating habits

By the age of three, your child is no longer just eating milk or porridge - they are actively participating in family meals and developing their own preferences (and dislikes!). You may have already noticed that your child suddenly only wants to eat pasta without sauce or refuses vegetables.

Eating is much more than just eating: it means community, enjoyment, but sometimes also conflict. Your child is now learning how to handle cutlery, discover different flavours and express their own will.

How can you encourage healthy eating habits without causing stress at the dinner table? What to do if your child is fussy? And what does a balanced diet for small children look like?

18.1 Why children are sometimes fussy

Many small children have phases in which they suddenly reject certain foods or only want to eat one single dish.

💡 **Why are toddlers picky when it comes to food?**

✔ They discover their own will and want to have a say in decisions.

✔ They are sometimes afraid of new foods ("neophobia").

✔ They prefer familiar flavours and textures.

✓ They instinctively sense what their body needs (e.g. more carbohydrates during growth phases).

📌 **Important:** These phases are normal and nothing to worry about - almost all children go through a "fussy phase" at some point.

How can you deal with it?

✓ **Stay calm:** The more pressure you put on your child, the more he or she will block it.
✓ **Keep offering new foods**, but without forcing them.
✓ **Make food interesting through play:** "Would you like to try the red or yellow pepper strips?"
✓ **Let your child help:** Chop vegetables, stir - those who help with cooking often prefer to eat.

📌 **Tip:** Even if your child refuses a food, this can change at any time - it often takes 10-15 attempts before a child accepts a new food.

18.2 Shared meals as a family ritual

Eating is more than just nutrient intake - it's a social event. Shared meals strengthen the bond and help your child to develop eating habits.

Why are family meals important?

✓ Your child learns by imitation - it sees how you eat and adopts your behaviour.
✓ They develop a natural relationship with food, without pressure or coercion.
✓ They associate food with positive experiences and not with stress.

Tips for stress-free family meals:

✓ **Sit down at the table together**, without distraction from the TV or toys.
✓ **Avoid pressure:** "Eat at least three more spoons!" often leads to resistance.
✓ **Allow independence:** Even if your child spills - they want to eat on their own.
✓ **Make mealtimes relaxed:** Tell each other something nice instead of arguing.

📌 **Tip:** A regular eating rhythm helps to regulate your child's hunger - fixed breakfast, lunch and dinner times are ideal.

18.3 Sugar, snacks and alternatives

Many parents wonder how much sugar is okay for small children - and how to find healthy alternatives.

How much sugar is allowed?

- The WHO recommends **as little sugar as possible** for small children.

- Hidden sugar is often found in yoghurts, muesli and fruit juices.

- Occasional sweets are okay - but they should not become a habit.

Healthy alternatives to sugary snacks:

✓ Instead of fruit juice: **Diluted apple juice or water with pieces of fruit**

✓ Instead of sweets: **Fruit slices, dates, homemade muesli bars**

✓ Instead of sweetened yoghurt: **natural yoghurt with fresh berries**

✓ Instead of biscuits: **rice cakes or home-baked oat biscuits**

📌 **Tip:** Your child doesn't have to give up sweets completely - it's important to be conscious about how you use them.

18.4 Eating as a game of discovery

Eating should be fun! Children discover food with all their senses - by seeing, feeling, smelling and tasting.

💡 **How can you make the food fun?**

✓ **Colourful plates:** Offer a selection of different colours (red tomatoes, green cucumbers, yellow peppers).

✓ **Fun shapes:** Cut bread or fruit into stars or hearts.

✓ **"Tasting plate":** Provide small portions of new foods - without pressure.

✓ **Finger food:** Children often prefer to eat with their hands rather than cutlery.

📌 **Tip:** The more your child is allowed to decide for themselves, the more likely they are to try new things.

18.5 What to do if your child hardly eats?

Some toddlers only eat tiny amounts - this can be unsettling for parents.

💡 **When should you worry?**

▶ Your child is losing a lot of weight or has stopped growing.

▶ It consistently refuses whole food groups.

▶ They regularly have digestive problems or stomach ache.

▶ They have hardly any appetite for a long time.

📌 **In most cases, loss of appetite is harmless!**

Tips if your child eats little:

✓ **Pay attention to your child's feeling of fullness:** They usually know how much they need themselves.

✓ **Avoid snacks just before meals.**

✓ **Don't worry if your child doesn't eat much one day - they will often make up for it the next day.**

✓ **Let your child set the pace.**

📌 **Tip:** If you are unsure, talk to your paediatrician - but the appetite usually regulates itself.

Conclusion: Healthy eating habits develop through play

Eating in infancy is an exciting learning process. Your child develops their own preferences, discovers new foods and learns to eat independently.

🍸 **What you can take with you:**

✓ It's normal to have a fussy phase - be patient and keep offering new foods.

✓ Shared meals are valuable for the whole family.

✓ A conscious approach to sugar is better than a strict ban.

✓ Food can be playful - colours, shapes and finger food make it exciting.

✓ Every child has their own pace - coercion and pressure only make eating unpleasant.

With patience, fun and a relaxed approach to nutrition, you can help your child develop healthy eating habits for life. 💜 🗨 🖤

19. four years - preparation for pre-school

At the age of four, an exciting new phase begins for your child. They are no longer a toddler, but a real preschooler! They can now concentrate better, ask specific questions, think more logically and are increasingly interested in letters, numbers and socialising with other children.

You may notice that your child is becoming more independent and is proud to learn new things. At the same time, however, they still need a lot of support and loving guidance to expand their knowledge and prepare for the next big step - pre-school.

How can you encourage your child in a playful way without putting pressure on them? Which skills are particularly important at this age? And how can you prepare your child to be a "big pre-schooler" soon?

19.1 First concentration exercises

At the age of four, your child can already concentrate better on one task - but not for as long as a schoolchild. They quickly switch from one activity to the next, especially when something gets boring.

🍸 **How long can a four-year-old concentrate?**

✓ Usually **10-15 minutes per task**, after which they need a break.

✓ Some children are attentive for longer if they are particularly interested in something.

✓ Movement helps - children learn better if they can run or jump in between.

How can you promote concentration?

✓ **Plan quiet play times** when your child is doing puzzles or colouring.

✓ **Avoid sensory overload** - a tidy environment helps them to concentrate on one thing at a time.

✓ **Combine movement and concentration** - e.g. jumping games with numbers or letters.

✓ **Have patience!** The attention span grows over time.

📌 **Tip:** Simple concentration games such as "I see something you don't see" or memory games encourage attention in a playful way.

19.2 Dealing with rules and consequences

Four-year-olds have a better understanding of rules - but they also like to test them! Your child knows that they can't just cross the road or that they should tidy up after playing. Nevertheless, they will sometimes 'forget' or deliberately try to see if you are really consistent.

Why are rules important?
✓ They give your child security and structure.
✓ They help to develop social skills (e.g. being considerate, waiting, sharing).
✓ They prepare your child for school, where certain rules apply.

How do you enforce rules lovingly?

✓ **Be consistent but patient:** A "no" should remain a "no" - but without penalties.
✓ **Explain the rules in simple terms:** "We wash our hands because we wash away the germs."
✓ **Use visual reminders:** A picture with a "clean up time" can help.
✓ **Let your child have a say:** Children are more likely to stick to rules if they are allowed to have a say ("Should we brush our teeth first or read the story first?").

➤ **Tip:** A simple and consistent daily routine helps to reinforce rules - such as fixed mealtimes and bedtimes.

19.3 Why painting and handicrafts are so important

You may have noticed that your child draws more purposefully at the age of four - they no longer just make doodles, but recognisable shapes and figures. Painting, cutting and crafting are not only creative activities, but also important preparation for later writing skills.

Why does painting and crafting promote development?
✓ It improves fine motor skills - important for writing later on.
✓ It strengthens concentration and stamina.
✓ It promotes creativity and the ability to express oneself.
✓ It helps to express feelings - children often paint what moves them.

Simple craft ideas for four-year-olds:

✓ **Painting with finger paints** - children love to feel colours with their hands.
✓ **Cutting exercises with children's scissors** - strengthens finger strength.
✓ **Kneading and moulding with salt dough or modelling clay** - promotes fine motor skills.
✓ **Colouring in first letters or numbers and tracing them.**

➤ **Tip:** Hang up your child's artwork - it boosts their self-confidence!

19.4 Developing motor skills

At the age of four, your child will become increasingly skilful in their movements. They can run, jump, climb and even stand on one leg. Gross and fine motor skills develop in parallel and prepare your child for writing, handicrafts and sporting activities.

What motor skills does a four-year-old already have?

✓ Run safely and stop suddenly.

✓ Stand on one leg (for a few seconds).

✓ Catch and throw a ball.

✓ Walking up and down stairs alternately.

✓ Eat with cutlery without spilling too much.

How can you promote motor development?

✓ **Incorporate exercise into everyday life:** Take the stairs instead of the lift.

✓ **Set up an obstacle course in the garden or living room.**

✓ **Balance on the floor with chalk or play hopscotch.**

✓ **Try out simple sports for the first time:** Riding a balance bike, jumping rope or balancing on a low tree trunk.

📌 **Tip:** Physical activity is important - children need exercise to develop healthily!

19.5 Learning social skills in a group

In the fourth year of life, social interaction becomes increasingly important. While toddlers often still play side by side (parallel play), four-year-olds start to play together and make their first friends.

What happens in this phase?

✓ Children start to **play together**, not just next to each other.

✓ They learn to **share and wait** - even if this is still difficult at times.

✓ The first **conflicts arise** because they want to get their own way.

✓ They develop **empathy** - "Oh, you're sad? Do you want me to help you?"

How can you promote social skills?

✓ **Support role play:** Playing with dolls, cars or figures helps to re-enact social situations.

✓ **Praise for friendly behaviour:** "That was nice of you to share your toy!"

✓ **Solve conflicts together:** Don't always intervene immediately, but let your child find a solution themselves.

✓ **Read books about friendship:** Stories help to understand social behaviour.

📌 **Tip:** Your child doesn't have to play with everyone - but they should learn to be polite and resolve conflicts fairly.

Conclusion: Your child is making great progress - playfully and with joy!

At the age of four, your child develops important skills that prepare them for pre-school. They can concentrate better, understand rules, become more confident with their motor skills and start to make real friends.

 What you can take away:

✓ The ability to concentrate grows - but playful encouragement is the best way.

✓ Rules and consequences help your child to feel safe.

✓ Colouring, arts and crafts and movement are important preparations for school.

✓ Social skills develop through joint games and conflict resolution.

Enjoy this special time - your child is now a curious, creative and eager to learn preschooler! 🖤 ✨

20. preschool children - the last big developmental step

At the age of five, your child is in the last phase before school. They are curious, eager to learn and want to do more and more on their own. At the same time, their social understanding is growing - they understand better how rules work, can maintain friendships and are beginning to deal with numbers, letters and their own role in the world.

Starting pre-school is an exciting time: your child is no longer a toddler, but is developing into a self-confident little person with lots of questions, ideas and needs. In this chapter, you will find out how you can prepare your child for school in the best possible way - playfully and without pressure.

20.1 How gaming behaviour changes

At the age of five, the way your child plays changes. While younger children still often play side by side (parallel play), your child is now immersed more and more in role-playing games and can spend longer periods of time on one thing.

Typical play changes at pre-school age:

✓ **Co-operative games:** Your child can now play in a group and understand rules.

✓ **Role-playing games become more complex:** They act out everyday situations (doctor's surgery, school, shop).

✓ **Parlour games become more interesting:** Your child can play their first simple board games with rules.

✓ **Creative play increases:** they paint, do handicrafts and invent their own stories.

✦ **Tip:** Games with fixed rules help your child to practise patience and learn to lose - an important step in their emotional development.

20.2 Numbers, letters and first attempts at writing

Many pre-school children are interested in letters and numbers - especially if they recognise them in everyday life (e.g. on street signs or packaging).

How does interest in letters and numbers manifest itself?

✓ Your child recognises and names individual letters ("That's an M for mummy!").

✓ They write their first letters - often in reverse (that's normal!).

✓ They count things out ("1, 2, 3 apples!").

✓ He shows interest in his name and tries to write it.

How can you support your child?

✓ **Offer letters to trace** - with sand, finger paints or pens.

✓ **Count everyday objects together:** "How many spoons are on the table?"

✓ **Let your child discover letters through play:** In books, on signs or when playing with magnetic letters.

✓ **Avoid pressure!** Your child doesn't have to be able to read or write yet - everything comes with time.

➤ **Tip:** Children learn by having fun - letters and numbers are great for integrating into movement games or songs!

20.3 Strengthening self-confidence

At the age of five, your child is more self-confident, but still needs your support to believe in themselves and overcome challenges.

What boosts your child's self-confidence?

✓ **Praise for effort, not just for the result:** "You really made an effort to build the tower!"

✓ **Encourage independence:** Your child can now set the table, get dressed or do small tasks on their own.

✓ **Encourage them:** If your child is unsure ("I can't do it!"), encourage them: "Just try it, I'll help you if you want."

✓ **Take feelings seriously:** Even if something seems small - it can be a big challenge for your child.

➤ **Tip:** The more successful experiences your child has, the more self-confident they will become. Let them try things out, even if they don't work straight away.

20.4 How to prepare your child for school

Many parents ask themselves how they can best prepare their child for school. The good news is that children learn best through play - strict pre-school training is not necessary.

What skills are important for starting school?

✓ **Social skills:** Listening, finding your way in a group, showing consideration for others.

✓ **Concentration:** Concentrating on a task for 10-15 minutes.

✓ **Fine motor skills:** Knowing how to use scissors and a pencil.

✓ **Independence:** Putting on a jacket, tying shoes, going to the toilet.

✓ **Language skills:** Retelling stories, understanding simple instructions.

This is how you can support your child:

✓ **Play games with rules:** "I see what you don't see", memory or simple board games.

✓ **Use everyday situations:** Your child can recognise numbers when shopping or discover letters on signs.

✓ **Assign small tasks:** setting the table, tying shoes - this strengthens self-confidence and independence.

✓ **Crafting, painting and cutting together:** This trains fine motor skills and creativity.

📌 **Tip:** Your child doesn't have to be able to write or do maths before starting school - it's enough if they are interested in new things and enjoy learning.

20.5 The last day at daycare - an emotional farewell

Leaving daycare can be a big moment for your child - it means the transition to a new stage of life. Some children are looking forward to school, others have mixed feelings.

💡 **How can you prepare your child to say goodbye?**

✓ **Talk to them about the transition:** "School is starting soon - it's going to be exciting!"

✓ **Reminisce about good times at nursery:** Look at photos or handmade crafts.

✓ **Organise a little farewell:** A celebration or a day out with daycare friends can help to make the transition a positive one.

✓ **Emphasise the anticipation of school:** "You can discover so many new things at school!"

📌 **Tip:** Some children are afraid of change - give them time to get used to the idea and answer any questions about the school.

Conclusion: Your child is ready for the next adventure!

The last year before school is an exciting time full of new skills, growing independence and emotional development. Your child becomes more curious, braver and begins to prepare for the start of school.

💡 **What you can take with you:**

✓ Playing is the best preparation for school - learning happens through play!

✓ Your child will become more independent - give them tasks that they can complete on their own.

✓ Letters, numbers and concentration can be easily integrated into everyday life.

✓ A self-confident child goes to school with more joy - encourage them!

✓ Leaving daycare can be emotional - accompany your child with understanding and anticipation.

At the age of five, your child is ready for new challenges. A new adventure is about to begin - and you can be proud of how far your child has already come! 🤍 ✨ 📖

21. social behaviour - making friends and learning to share

At the age of five, your child begins to form deeper social relationships. It's no longer just about playing together, but also about real friendships. Your child learns to compromise, share and resolve conflicts - all of which are important skills for starting school and later in life.

But socialising can also be challenging: Why do some children find it hard to share? How can parents help if their child struggles to make friends? And how can you help a child to be empathetic and considerate?

In this chapter, you will learn how to support your child in their social development and help them to become good friends.

21.1 Why sharing is difficult for children

Sharing is one of the most important social skills - but it has to be learnt first. Favourite toys in particular are often vehemently defended.

Why do children find it difficult to share?

✓ Ownership is a big issue for children - they are just learning what "mine" and "yours" mean.
✓ They are afraid of not getting something back.
✓ They see things as an extension of their identity ("My cuddly toy is only mine!").
✓ They are not yet able to empathise with others ("I want this - why should I give it away?").

How can you encourage sharing?

✓ **Be patient:** Sharing is a learning process - don't expect it to work right away.
✓ **Set an example:** Show that you like to share things yourself ("Would you like a piece of my apple?").
✓ **Explain why sharing is important**: "If you share your building blocks, you can build a big tower together."
✓ **Use games that require sharing:** Jigsaw puzzles or painting together encourage cooperative behaviour.
✓ **Praise when it works:** "That was great that you shared your car with your friend!"

➴ **Tip:** Don't force your child to share, but explain the benefits to them - they will be willing to do so over time.

21.2 Mine or yours? Understanding ownership

A frequent topic of dispute among children is: "That's mine!" Especially in groups such as daycare centres or on the playground, there are often conflicts about who owns a particular toy.

What does "property" mean for children?

✓ Children first learn to distinguish between communal and private property.
✓ They need to understand that some things belong to "everyone" (e.g. toys in the daycare centre).
✓ They learn that swapping and borrowing can also be fun.

How can you support your child?

✓ **Explain ownership clearly:** "The toys in the kindergarten belong to everyone, your cuddly toy belongs only to you."

✓ **Help your child to be fair:** "You can use the car first, then your friend can have it."

✓ **Let your child decide:** It's okay if they don't want to share certain things - but they should be able to offer alternatives.

📌 **Tip:** The concept of ownership develops over time - your child must first learn what "borrowing", "swapping" and "sharing" really mean.

21.3 First friendships: How children socialise

At the age of five, children develop real friendships - they have favourite playmates and always want to see certain friends again.

🏆 How do you recognise that your child is building friendships?

✓ They name certain children as "best friends".

✓ They want to have dates with their friends.

✓ They look after others and notice when someone is sad.

✓ They enthusiastically share experiences from daycare or the playground.

How can you support your child in making friends?

✓ **Encourage appointments with other children.**

✓ **Help with socialising:** "Would you like to play ball with the other children?"

✓ **Show your child how to approach others politely.**

✓ **Let your child decide who they want to play with - not every child gets on with everyone.**

📌 **Tip:** Friendships often develop from shared interests - support your child in finding out what they enjoy.

21.4 Resolving conflicts between children

Disputes are normal at this age - whether over toys, seating or who goes first. But conflicts are important because they help children to find solutions and develop socially.

🏆 Why do children argue?

✓ They test boundaries.

✓ They practise asserting their will.

✓ They don't yet have enough strategies for conflict resolution.

How can you help without solving everything?

✓ **Remain neutral:** Don't be a "referee" straight away, but encourage your child to find a solution themselves.

✓ **Help them find words:** "Can you tell him why you're sad?"

✓ **Mediate if necessary:** "You both want to play with the car - how can you sort this out?"

✓ **Praise good conflict behaviour:** "That was great that you came to an agreement yourselves!"

Tip: Children need time to find fair solutions - don't expect things to work out immediately.

21.5 Promoting empathy - why compassion is important

Empathy means putting yourself in someone else's shoes - a skill that develops from pre-school age. Your child now begins to understand how others feel and why consideration is important.

How does empathy manifest itself in children?

✓ They comfort other children when they are sad.

✓ They say: "I'll help you!" or "Do you want to join in?"

✓ They notice when someone is excluded.

How can you promote empathy?

✓ **Naming feelings:** "Look, your friend is sad - what could we do to cheer him up?"

✓ **Be a role model:** Children learn compassion by seeing how we treat others.

✓ **Read books about friendship and feelings.**

✓ **Saying thank you and apologising**: "Thank you for helping me!" shows appreciation.

Tip: Empathy grows over time - your child still needs to practise empathising with others.

Conclusion: Social learning is a process

At the age of five, your child is making huge progress in social interaction. They learn to make friends, share, resolve conflicts and empathise with others.

What you can take with you:

✓ **Sharing has to be learnt - be patient!**

✓ **Ownership is an important topic - your child learns what "mine" and "yours" mean.**

✓ **Friendships are made through shared experiences - encourage socialising.**

✓ **Disputes are normal - support your child in finding solutions.**

✓ **Empathy develops slowly - your child needs role models and time.**

Social behaviour is a long learning process, but with your support your child will grow up to be an empathetic and considerate little person! 🖤 👫

---

22. media consumption - dealing with television, tablet and co.

In today's digital world, media is omnipresent - even for children. Whereas in the past we might have only been able to watch a few TV programmes a day, today children have countless digital offerings at their fingertips: TV, tablet, smartphone, streaming services, video games and much more.

But how much screen time is healthy? When should a child even come into contact with digital media? And how can you encourage responsible use of TV, tablets and other devices? In this chapter, you will learn how to integrate media into your child's everyday life in a sensible way without it becoming their main occupation.

22.1 When is the right time for media?

Many parents wonder when their child should watch television or play with a tablet for the first time.

💡 **Experts' recommendations:**
✓ Children under the **age of 2** should have as little screen time as possible - they learn best through real play and social interaction.
✓ From **2-3 years**, the first child-friendly content can be introduced in small doses (e.g. 10-15 minutes a day).
✓ From **4-6 years, a maximum of 30-45 minutes per day** is recommended, depending on the type of content.

👉 **Important:** Digital media are not "babysitters" - they should always be accompanied by conversations and real play.

22.2 How much screen time is healthy?

The right amount of media consumption depends on the age and daily structure of the child.

💡 **Recommended screen time per age group:**
✓ **Under 2 years old:** Preferably no media or only occasionally together with parents.
✓ **2-4 years:** Max. 15-30 minutes per day, e.g. a short children's programme.
✓ **4-6 years:** Max. 30-45 minutes per day, divided into meaningful sections.
✓ **6-9 years:** Up to 60 minutes per day, with clear rules.

👉 **Tip:** Instead of "How much?", the question "How sensible?" is more important - it depends on what your child consumes.

22.3 Selecting child-friendly content

Not every programme or app is suitable for children - even cartoon series can sometimes be too exciting or scary.

💡 **What should you look out for in children's media?**
✓ **Age-appropriate content:** No violence, overwhelming themes or quick cuts.
✓ **Calm stories with simple plots:** Series with soft colour tones and slow narration are better than hectic cartoons.
✓ **Interactive content instead of passive entertainment**: Apps in which the child can participate promote learning.
✓ **No adverts**: Many children's apps are full of adverts - look out for ad-free content.

Recommended media for preschool children:

📺 **Series:** "Die Sendung mit der Maus", "Leo Lausemaus", "Peppa Wutz", "Sesame Street"
🔲 **Apps:** "Sendung mit der Maus App", "Anton" (learning app), "Book Creator" (for creating

stories)

🎮 **Games:** Child-friendly movement games or simple educational games

📌 **Tip:** Parents should always have a say in what their children watch - it's best to watch it together and talk about it.

22.4 Alternatives to digital media

Children don't necessarily need media to entertain themselves - there are many great alternatives that encourage creativity and movement.

💡 **What can you offer instead of screen time?**

✓ **Creative games:** Painting, crafting, modelling or making up your own stories.

✓ **Exercise:** A walk, a ball game or a ride on a balance bike.

✓ **Reading aloud:** Children love stories - and it encourages language and imagination.

✓ **Free play:** Children learn the most when they are simply allowed to play.

📌 **Tip:** A "media-free zone" in the home (e.g. the children's room) helps to limit consumption.

22.5 Parents as role models in media consumption

Children learn by imitation - if you are constantly on your mobile phone, your child will want to be too.

💡 **How can you set an example of healthy media use?**

✓ **Consciously take mobile phone breaks:** Your child will notice if you keep looking at the screen.

✓ **Introduce media-free family times:** No screens at mealtimes or before bedtime.

✓ **Watch together instead of consuming alone:** Talk to your child about what they are watching.

✓ **Show alternatives:** Read a book yourself instead of scrolling on your mobile phone - this will encourage your child to do the same.

📌 **Tip:** If your child complains because they are not allowed to use a tablet or watch TV, a clear and loving attitude will help: "Now is playtime, TV is for later."

Conclusion: A conscious approach to media is crucial

Digital media is part of our world - children should learn to use it sensibly instead of avoiding it completely. The key lies in a good balance between media consumption, exercise, creative play and social interaction.

💡 **What you can take away:**

✓ Children under the age of 2 don't need media - they learn through real play.

✓ Toddlers should spend a maximum of 30-45 minutes a day with digital media.

✓ Choose **child-friendly content** and avoid fast, loud and violent media.

✓ **Digital media is no substitute for free play** - real experiences are more important.

✓ **Parents are role models!** Your use of mobile phones influences your child.

A conscious approach to media ensures that your child uses it sensibly - without it replacing real life. 💜 ▦ ▭

23. promoting independence - small tasks in everyday life

At the age of five, your child will become increasingly independent. They want to do many things on their own and feel proud when they can complete tasks independently. At the same time, they are often still impatient, easily frustrated or need encouragement to take on challenges.

Independence is an important skill that prepares your child for school and later life. But how can you support them without overburdening them? What small tasks can they take on? And how can you teach them responsibility in a playful way?

23.1 Why children want to help

Many parents are familiar with this situation: the child really wants to pour the milk, set the table or tie their own shoes - but it often takes longer or goes wrong. Nevertheless, it is important to encourage this initiative.

💡 **Why is independence important?**

✓ It strengthens self-confidence - your child feels competent.

✓ It promotes problem-solving skills - through trial and error and practice.

✓ It helps to develop frustration tolerance - not everything works right away.

✓ It makes your child fit for everyday life - they learn to take responsibility.

📌 **Tip:** Children learn through repetition. Even if your child takes longer or makes mistakes, it is important to let them try things out for themselves.

23.2 Small household chores for preschool children

Children love to be involved in everyday life. There are lots of small tasks that your child can take on - and that develop important skills at the same time.

Which tasks are age-appropriate?

✓ **From 2-3 years:**

- Clear away toys

- Helping to lay the table

- Sort socks

✓ **From 4 years:**

- Wipe the table

- Watering plants

- Carrying small purchases

✓ **From 5 years:**

- Make his bed

- Bringing your own plate into the kitchen

- Dressing yourself

📌 **Tip:** Turn the tasks into a playful challenge ("Can you manage to collect all the red building blocks?").

23.3 Be patient if it is not perfect

Parents are often tempted to do tasks for their child because it is quicker or looks more "right". But children need practice to do things independently.

💡 **Why are mistakes important?**

✓ They help the child to learn through experience.
✓ They show that perfection is not the goal.
✓ They encourage perseverance - your child does not give up immediately.

How can you stay patient?

✓ **Don't expect perfection:** a crooked bed is also a made bed.
✓ **Praise the attempt, not just the result:** "You made a real effort!"
✓ **Avoid criticism**: "Oh no, you did that wrong!" discourages your child.
✓ **Be a role model:** show that you also make mistakes ("Oops, I spilt the milk. I'll just wipe it up.").

📌 **Tip:** Let your child make small mistakes - they will learn from them and become more skilful over time.

23.4 Giving freedom of choice: What children can already do

Children learn independence by being allowed to make decisions. The aim is not to let them decide completely freely, but to offer them age-appropriate choices.

💡 **Why are decisions important?**

✓ They strengthen self-confidence.
✓ They help to take responsibility.
✓ They promote logical thinking ("Which shoes are best in the rain?").

What decisions can your child make?

✓ **Choosing clothes**: "Would you like the blue or the red jacket?"
✓ **Helping to decide what to eat:** "Would you prefer a banana or an apple?"
✓ **Helping to organise the day:** "Do we want to paint or read a book first?"

📌 **Tip:** Too many choices overwhelm children. Limit the choice to two or three options.

23.5 The right way to deal with responsibility

At the age of five, your child can already take responsibility for small things. This helps them to feel needed and build up their self-confidence.

💡 **How can you encourage responsibility?**
✓ **Let your child take on tasks:** "Can you remember to set the table today?"
✓ **Give them real responsibility:** a small project of their "own" (e.g. caring for a plant).
✓ **Explain why responsibility is important:** "If you tidy up your toys, you'll find them again more quickly tomorrow."

📌 **Tip:** Responsibility grows with positive experiences - encourage your child and celebrate successes!

Conclusion: independence grows through practice and trust

At the age of five, your child is ready to take on more responsibility and take care of small tasks more independently. They want to be taken seriously and feel competent.

💡 **What you can take away:**
✓ Children want to help - give them small, doable tasks.
✓ Mistakes are part of learning - encourage your child to try things out for themselves.
✓ Opportunities to make decisions boost self-confidence.
✓ Responsibility makes children proud - they learn that they can make a difference.

By involving your child in everyday life, you help them to become self-confident and independent. 🤍 👐 ✨

24. the first fears - what preoccupies children

At the age of five, your child has a vivid imagination - and it is precisely this imagination that can also trigger fears. While they may not have been afraid to go into dark rooms or try new things in the past, monsters may suddenly be lurking under the bed, separation anxiety may arise or insecurities about new situations may develop.

But fears are not just unpleasant - they are an important part of a child's development. They help your child to be careful and assess risks. At the same time, it is important that you help them to deal with their fears so that they don't get out of hand.

How do fears develop in children? What fears are typical at this age? And how can you support your child without minimising their worries?

24.1 Fear of the dark - How you can help

Many children are afraid of the dark - one of the most common fears at pre-school age. They are afraid of shadows, noises or the idea that "something is hiding" in their room.

💡 Why are children afraid of the dark?
✓ Their imagination develops strongly - they imagine things that are not there.
✓ Darkness means uncertainty - they can't see what's going on around them.
✓ Nightmares can intensify the fear.

What can you do?

✓ **Take the fear seriously:** "I understand that you feel uncomfortable when it's dark."
✓ **Leave a night light on:** A small lamp or a calming light can help.
✓ **Show your child that nothing is there:** Go into the room together and check.
✓ **Read positive bedtime stories:** Stories about brave children can help to overcome fear.

📌 **Tip:** Avoid phrases like "It's not that bad" - it's a real fear for your child!

24.2 Understanding nightmares and night terrors

Perhaps your child has woken up screaming in the middle of the night and could hardly be calmed down - a typical night terror. Or they have bad dreams that frighten them.

💡 What is the difference between nightmares and night terrors?
✓ **Nightmares** occur during REM sleep - your child often remembers them.
✓ **Night terrors** happen during a deep sleep phase - your child is confused and unresponsive.

How can you help?

✓ **For nightmares:** Stay calm, comfort your child and talk about the dream if they want to.
✓ **For night terrors:** Leave your child alone, they often wake up on their own and don't remember.
✓ **Ensure a relaxed evening routine:** Less exciting games and calm bedtime rituals help.

📌 **Tip:** Night terrors are often caused by overtiredness - a regular sleep rhythm can help.

24.3 Separation anxiety - How to accompany your child

Separation anxiety can occur at various stages of childhood - even at pre-school age. Some children find it difficult to say goodbye to mum or dad, whether at nursery, when playing with friends or when falling asleep.

💡 Why do children have separation anxiety?
✓ They are more aware of absence - they know you are really gone.
✓ They fear that something will happen while you are away.
✓ They are used to routine and change can cause uncertainty.

How can you support your child?

✓ **Clear, loving farewell rituals:** A fixed routine ("A kiss, a hug and a wave") provides security.

✓ **Avoid prolonged hesitation:** The longer it takes to say goodbye, the harder it is.

✓ **Reassure your child that you will be back:** "I'll pick you up after lunch."

✓ **Let them practise small separations:** first short periods alone with Grandma, then longer separations.

📌 **Tip:** If you remain calm and confident, your child will realise that everything is okay.

24.4 Fear of strangers and new situations

Some children are shy or afraid of new people and unfamiliar situations.

💡 **Why are children afraid of strangers?**

✓ They need time to get used to new people.

✓ They feel insecure in new environments.

✓ They are afraid of doing something wrong.

How can you encourage your child?

✓ **Give it time:** Not every child is immediately open - it can get used to new people slowly.

✓ **Prepare them for new situations:** Explain what is going to happen ("Today we are going to meet grandma's friends").

✓ **Be a role model:** If you approach people in a friendly manner, your child will imitate this.

✓ **Don't force it:** Your child shouldn't feel pressurised into talking to someone.

📌 **Tip:** Some children need longer to feel comfortable - give them the time they need.

24.5 Conveying trust and security

Fears are part of a child's development - but your child needs to learn that it is safe and that it can overcome fears.

💡 **How can you give your child confidence?**

✓ **Be a safe haven:** Your child needs to know that they can always come to you.

✓ **Take fears seriously, but don't reinforce them:** "I know you're scared, but you can do it!"

✓ **Show that fear can be overcome:** "Remember when you used to be afraid of dogs? Now you like them!"

✓ **Praise courage:** "I'm proud that you dared to go into the room on your own!"

📌 **Tip:** Your child doesn't have to be anxiety-free straight away - but they should know that they can learn to deal with anxiety with your help.

Conclusion: Fears are normal - and can be overcome

Fears are part of childhood and are often a sign of a growing imagination. It is important that you accompany your child, give them security and show them that they can overcome their fears.

💡 **What you can take with you:**

✓ Fear of the dark is normal - a night light or a calming ritual can help.

✓ Nightmares and night terrors are not dangerous - but they can be stressful.

✓ Separation anxiety can come in phases - fixed rituals and security help.

✓ Fear of strangers and new situations is normal - your child needs time.

✓ Courage grows with experience - encourage your child to overcome fears.

Your child will learn that they are safe - with your support they can overcome any fear. 🖤

25. exercise and sport - why activity is so important

Children have a natural urge to move - they run, climb, jump, romp and discover the world with their bodies. Exercise is essential for your child's healthy physical and mental development. It not only strengthens muscles and bones, but also promotes concentration, self-confidence and social skills.

But in this day and age, when many children are spending more and more time with tablets, television or video games, exercise is becoming increasingly important. How can you motivate your child to be more active? Which sports are suitable for preschoolers? And how can you playfully integrate exercise into everyday life?

25.1 Romping, climbing, running - understanding the urge to move

Children have a natural need to move around. They don't like to sit still, climb on anything they find and jump around when they're happy.

💡 **Why is exercise so important?**

✓ It strengthens muscles and bones and promotes healthy posture.

✓ It improves coordination, motor skills and balance.

✓ It supports brain development - exercise promotes concentration.

✓ It helps to release excess energy and reduce stress.

✓ It makes children more self-confident and helps to overcome fears.

📌 **Tip:** Instead of trying to curb your child's urge to move, consciously integrate movement into everyday life.

25.2 Which sports are suitable for small children?

At the age of five, children are ready for their first structured sports - but without any pressure to perform! The important thing is that the exercise is fun.

💡 **Which sports are ideal for preschool children?**

🤸 **Children's gymnastics:** Promotes coordination, balance and social skills.

⚽ **Football:** Helps with teamwork, stamina and motor skills.

Children's yoga: Improves posture, concentration and relaxation.

Cycling or running bikes: Trains balance and strengthens leg muscles.

Swimming: An important skill that strengthens the entire musculature at the same time.

Judo or karate for children: Promotes body control, discipline and self-confidence.

Tip: Try out different activities - every child has different preferences!

25.3 Promoting motor skills through movement games

Children don't have to go to a sports club to get enough exercise. Simple exercise games at home or in the playground are enough to improve motor skills and body awareness.

Movement games for at home and outdoors:

✓ **Jumping games (e.g. heaven and hell)** - trains jumping ability and balance.

✓ **Catching games** - promote endurance and speed.

✓ **Balancing exercises (on kerbs or tree trunks)** - improve balance.

✓ **Throwing and catching balls** - improves hand-eye coordination.

✓ **Obstacle course with cushions or chairs** - ideal for rainy days.

✓ **Dance and movement games with music** - fun and exercises the whole body.

Tip: Children love competitions - incorporate playful challenges ("How many times can you hop on one leg?").

25.4 Why children can't sit still

"My child just can't sit still!" - Many parents often hear this sentence, especially when it comes to eating, listening at nursery or reading aloud. But this is completely normal!

Why do preschool children find it difficult to sit still?

✓ Their brains are constantly processing new impressions - movement helps them to process these.

✓ They have a lot of energy - movement is an outlet for them.

✓ Their bodies need movement to develop healthily.

✓ They learn best by actively doing, not by passively listening.

How can you deal with it?

✓ **Accept the natural urge to move:** Your child doesn't always have to sit still.

✓ **Incorporate movement into everyday life:** Take a short movement break before eating or reading aloud.

✓ **Let your child learn actively:** letters and numbers can be practised by jumping or singing.

Tip: Movement increases concentration - short movement sessions even help you to listen better afterwards.

25.5 Playing outside vs. playing inside

Playing outside has many advantages - it offers more space for movement, fresh air and the opportunity to interact with other children. But there are also creative opportunities for movement indoors.

💡 Why is outdoor play so important?

✓ Children have more space to run, climb and romp around.

✓ The fresh air strengthens the immune system.

✓ There is more natural movement outside - e.g. jumping over puddles or climbing trees.

✓ Experiencing nature encourages creativity and imagination.

What to do when the weather is bad?

✓ **Movement games indoors:** Dancing, yoga, cushion courses or jumping jacks.

✓ **Visit indoor playgrounds or swimming pools.**

✓ **Try out a children's fitness programme:** There are many online programmes with exercise videos for children.

📌 **Tip:** Whether indoors or outdoors - the main thing is exercise!

Conclusion: Exercise is the key to healthy development

Children need exercise to develop in a physically, mentally and emotionally healthy way. Whether it's sport, free romping or small movement games - the main thing is that movement is fun and becomes a natural part of everyday life.

💡 What you can take with you:

✓ Exercise is essential for physical and mental development.

✓ Children need at least **1-2 hours of active exercise per day**.

✓ Sports such as **gymnastics, swimming or cycling** are ideal for preschool children.

✓ Exercise games at home or outside promote motor skills and coordination.

✓ Outdoor play is particularly important - but there are also lots of ideas for exercise indoors.

The more your child enjoys exercise, the more active they will remain - an important foundation stone for a healthy life! 🖤 🚴 🏃

26. storytelling - the magic of fantasy

Children love stories - they immerse them in strange worlds, stimulate their imagination and help them to understand the world around them. With just a few words, you can take your child on an adventure in which dragons are defeated, treasures are found and friendships are made.

But storytelling is much more than just entertainment: it promotes language development, strengthens the bond between parent and child and helps to process emotions. Whether reading aloud, telling stories or inventing stories together - fantasy stories are a valuable part of childhood.

How can you get your child excited about stories? Why is reading aloud so important? And how can you make up your own stories together with your child?

26.1 Why children love stories

Children have a natural curiosity for stories. They love to immerse themselves in new worlds, identify with the characters and experience adventures in their imagination.

💡 **Why are stories so important for children?**

✓ They promote linguistic development and vocabulary.

✓ They help to better understand feelings and social situations.

✓ They stimulate the imagination and allow children to be creative.

✓ They convey values and show solutions to problems.

📌 **Tip:** Children don't just listen to stories passively - they actively experience them and learn a lot about themselves and the world in the process!

26.2 Storytelling, reading aloud or audio books?

Parents often ask themselves whether it is better to read stories to their child, tell them or keep them occupied with audio books. The answer is: all three options are valuable - in different ways.

💡 **Which form is suitable and when?**

📖 **Reading aloud:**

✓ Promotes language development and listening skills.

✓ Gives the child a sense of security by spending time together.

✓ Helps to learn new words and sentence structures.

🎤 **Free storytelling:**

✓ Stimulates the child's imagination.

✓ Encourages creative imagination.

✓ Offers the opportunity to incorporate personal experiences into stories.

🎧 **Audio books:**

✓ A good addition when parents don't have time to read aloud.

✓ Support listening and understanding of more complex stories.

✓ Can be a great activity when travelling.

📌 **Tip:** A mixture of reading aloud, storytelling and audio books is best - this will give your child a variety of stimuli.

26.3 Encourage creativity through your own stories

Children have an incredible imagination - so why not make up your own stories together? This not only boosts creativity, but also gives your child the opportunity to express their thoughts and feelings.

How can you make up stories together?

✓ **Storytelling games:** One sentence starts the story, then everyone takes it in turn.

✓ **Dice stories:** Roll the dice for characters, places and events and build them into a story.

✓ **Pictures as inspiration:** Look at a picture and think about the story behind it.

✓ **Incorporate characters from everyday life:** Cuddly toys, favourite toys or everyday objects can become heroes.

🖈 **Tip:** There is no "right" or "wrong" story - the important thing is that your child enjoys telling it!

26.4 What children can learn from fairy tales

Fairy tales have been part of our culture for centuries - but many parents wonder whether classic fairy tales with witches, evil stepmothers or talking animals are still up to date.

Why are fairy tales valuable?

✓ They convey values such as courage, friendship and justice.

✓ They help children to distinguish between good and evil.

✓ They show that challenges can be overcome.

✓ They encourage fantasy and imagination.

How can you tell fairy tales in a child-friendly way?

✓ **Choose age-appropriate fairy tales:** Not every fairy tale is suitable for all ages.

✓ **Talk about the story:** What did the child like? Was there a part that they found scary?

✓ **Change the story if necessary**: A fairy tale doesn't have to be told exactly as it is in the book - you can tone it down or change it.

🖈 **Tip:** Modern fairy tale books often offer a child-friendly, gentler version of the classic stories.

26.5 Role-playing games as an expression of fantasy

Children love to slip into other roles - be it as a knight, princess, fireman or vet. Role play is a wonderful way of bringing stories to life and practising social skills at the same time.

Why are role-playing games so important?

✓ They encourage creativity and imagination.

✓ They help to process experiences ("I play daycare centre").

✓ They train social skills and empathy.

✓ They give children the opportunity to slip into a different role and try themselves out.

How can you support role-playing games?

✓ **Offer props:** Dress-up boxes, stuffed animals or everyday objects as "magic wands".

✓ **Let your child take the lead:** They determine the story - you play along.

✓ **Combine role play with real experiences:** Your child can play doctor after having been to the paediatrician.

Tip: Children learn by playing - role play is a wonderful way to develop imagination and social skills.

Conclusion: Stories are more than just entertainment - they are a key to development

Whether reading aloud, telling or inventing your own stories - storytelling is a valuable part of childhood. It strengthens language, encourages imagination and creates a special bond between parent and child.

What you can take away:

✓ Children love stories because they help them to understand the world.

✓ Reading aloud, storytelling and audio books each have their own advantages.

✓ Making up your own stories encourages creativity and the ability to express yourself.

✓ Fairy tales are timeless - if they are told in a child-friendly way.

✓ Role play is a great way to bring stories to life.

With stories, your child not only grows into an imaginative world - they learn to express themselves, process emotions and empathise with others. So grab a book or make up your own story - the magical journey begins! 📖 ✦

27. develop anger outbursts and frustration tolerance

Tantrums are part of a child's development - you've probably experienced this many times. Your child is five years old, wants to get his way and sometimes can't stop himself. Whether it's about the wrong breakfast, a toy they didn't buy or tidying up the child's room - tantrums can be violent.

But anger is not just "bad behaviour" - it is an emotion that children first have to learn to regulate. Your child is going through major emotional changes during this phase. They are developing their own opinions, reaching their limits and are not yet able to process disappointments so easily.

How can you help your child deal with their anger? Why is frustration tolerance important? And how can you react lovingly but consistently to outbursts of anger?

27.1 Why children cannot control their feelings

For adults, it may seem incomprehensible why a child suddenly gets angry because the bread is broken in half. But from the child's point of view, the world has just gone off the rails.

Why are tantrums still normal at this age?

✓ Your child's brain is not yet fully developed - their ability to control themselves will only mature over time.

✓ They can sense emotions but cannot yet express them appropriately.

✓ They have a strong need for self-determination, but not always the ability to assert their wishes.

✓ They sometimes feel powerless and try to express their will through anger.

Tip: Tantrums are not manipulation - your child simply does not yet have a better strategy for dealing with frustration.

27.2 The right way to deal with anger

When your child throws a tantrum, it can be stressful - especially in public or after a long day. But your behaviour in such moments can make a big difference.

What helps with tantrums?

✓ **Stay calm** - your child can feel your energy. If you stay calm, it will calm down more quickly.
✓ **Name the emotion:** "I can see that you're really angry right now because you're not getting this."
✓ **Avoid long explanations in the acute situation** - children are not receptive in the anger phase.
✓ **Set clear boundaries:** "I understand that you're angry, but we won't hit you."
✓ **Offer an alternative:** "When you've calmed down, we can talk about it."

Tip: Anger is allowed - but dealing with it must be learnt. Your child is allowed to have feelings, but they must learn to express them appropriately.

27.3 How you can help your child to calm down

Every child is different - some calm down through physical contact, others need distance. It is important that you give your child the opportunity to regulate themselves.

What helps your child to calm down?

✓ **A calm voice and clear words:** "Take a deep breath, I'm here."
✓ **A safe place:** A cosy corner or a quiet room can help your child to relax.
✓ **Movement:** Sometimes it helps if your child works off their energy by jumping or running.
✓ **A favourite cuddly toy:** Children often calm down with something familiar.
✓ **Breathe and count:** "Breathe in slowly, then we'll count to five."

Tip: Not every child needs the same thing - observe what helps your child to regulate themselves.

27.4 Strategies for frustration tolerance

Frustration tolerance means being able to deal with failure and disappointment. This is one of the most important skills in life - but it needs to be practised.

How can you promote frustration tolerance?

✓ **Give your child small challenges:** A puzzle that is not solved immediately encourages them to keep at it.
✓ **Let your child find their own solutions:** "What can you do if the tower falls over?"
✓ **Praise the process, not just the result:** "You tried really hard - that was great!"

✓ **Avoid trying to solve everything immediately:** Your child is allowed to fail sometimes and learn from it.

✓ **Show that mistakes are okay:** "I made a mistake once too - then I'll try again!"

📌 **Tip:** Children who learn to deal with frustration are more self-confident and resilient later on.

27.5 Why it is important that children also hear "no"

Of course you want to see your child happy - but they also need to learn that not everything always goes their way. Saying 'no' is part of life and helps your child to deal with disappointment.

🏆 **Why is a clear "no" important?**

✓ It provides security - children need clear rules.

✓ It helps to deal with boundaries.

✓ It shows that wishes do not always have to be fulfilled immediately.

✓ It prevents spoiling and teaches patience.

How can you stay consistent?

✓ **Say "no" clearly and stick to it.**

✓ **Avoid long discussions.**

✓ **Offer alternatives:** "There's no ice cream today, but you can have a piece of fruit."

✓ **Show understanding for the disappointment:** "I can see that you're sad. That's okay."

📌 **Tip:** Children test boundaries - but if they feel that rules are reliable, this gives them security.

Conclusion: Anger is a normal emotion - children first have to learn how to deal with it

Tantrums are not malice, but an expression of strong feelings. Your child needs your support to learn to deal with frustration and disappointment.

🏆 **What you can take away:**

✓ Children cannot yet regulate their emotions like adults - outbursts of anger are normal.

✓ Stay calm when your child is angry - your attitude will help them to calm down.

✓ Anger is allowed, but dealing with it needs to be practised.

✓ Frustration tolerance is important - give your child small challenges and encourage them to persevere.

✓ Clear boundaries help - a consistent "no" is just as important as praise and encouragement.

When your child learns to deal with frustration and anger, it gives them tools for life. With your support, they will become more empathetic, patient and self-confident in dealing with difficult situations. 🖤 💧

28 The fifth birthday - A milestone

The fifth birthday is a very special moment in a child's life - and also for you as a parent. Your child is no longer a toddler, but well on the way to becoming an independent and curious preschooler. They are showing more self-confidence, taking responsibility for small tasks and have a growing idea of what they can and want to do.

At the same time, the fifth year of life brings with it many new challenges. Your child begins to engage more intensively with their environment, asks deeper questions and develops a stronger social awareness. How can you organise this special birthday? What developmental steps is your child taking now? And how can you prepare your child for the upcoming changes?

28.1 What a five-year-old can already do

At the age of five, your child has already undergone impressive development. Not only are they better at speaking, concentrating and understanding social rules, they are also becoming more physically skilful.

💡 **Typical skills of a five-year-old:**

✓ **Linguistic:** Tells longer stories, expresses himself well and asks lots of "why" questions.

✓ **Social:** Develops deeper friendships, understands rules better and can resolve conflicts.

✓ **Cognitive:** Can recognise colours, shapes, numbers and sometimes even some letters.

✓ **Motor:** Can hop on one leg, learn to ride a bike and do simple handicrafts themselves.

✓ **Emotional:** Understands emotions better, shows empathy and can empathise more with others.

🔖 **Tip:** Your child is now ready for bigger challenges - they love to try things out for themselves and be proud of their progress.

28.2 The development of self-confidence

At the age of five, your child's self-confidence grows enormously. They begin to understand what they are good at and are happy about recognition and success. At the same time, they are also more sensitive to criticism or failure.

💡 **How can you boost your child's self-confidence?**

✓ **Praise the process, not just the result:** "You made a real effort - great job!"

✓ **Let your child try things out on their own:** Even if they fail sometimes, they will still learn.

✓ **Show them that mistakes are okay:** "Everyone makes mistakes sometimes, it's part of the process."

✓ **Encourage them to try new things:** Whether it's sports, crafts or a new game - trying new things encourages courage.

🔖 **Tip:** Your child needs a sense of achievement, but also the experience that not everything always works straight away - this strengthens frustration tolerance.

28.3 The transition to preschool or school

Many children start pre-school at the age of five or are about to start school. This is a big change - and sometimes also a challenge.

How can you prepare your child for pre-school or school?

✓ **Talk positively about school:** "You'll learn exciting things there and make new friends!"

✓ **Encourage important skills through play:** Counting, reciting rhymes or playing with letters.

✓ **Practise small everyday skills:** Putting on a jacket alone, packing a rucksack, sitting at a table and listening.

✓ **Let your child make small decisions:** "Which T-shirt do you want to wear today?" - this strengthens self-confidence.

✦ **Tip:** A smooth transition to preschool or school is important - make your child curious, but also take away any fears.

28.4 How to make your birthday unforgettable

A fifth birthday is a big milestone - and should be celebrated! Many children now have their first concrete ideas about what their birthday should look like.

How can you organise a great birthday party?

✓ **Let your child help decide:** Would they like a theme party? Who should be invited?

✓ **Plan movement games:** Five-year-olds love to let off steam - a scavenger hunt, bouncy castle or simple competition games are ideal.

✓ **Create small rituals:** A birthday chair, a crown or a special cake will make the day unforgettable.

✓ **A mix of free play and supervised games:** Too many programme items can be stressful - a few set games, but also enough time for free play are perfect.

🎉 **Example of the organisation of a children's birthday party:**

☑ **15:00** - Arrival of the guests, free play

☑ **15:30** - Eating cake and unwrapping presents

☑ **16:00** - A scavenger hunt or a small game

☑ **16:30** - Free play or handicrafts

☑ **17:00** - Dinner or finger food

☑ **17:30** - Closing ritual (e.g. a small surprise for each child)

✦ **Tip:** A birthday party doesn't have to be perfect - the main thing is that your child feels special and has fun!

28.5 Looking back on five years of parenthood

The fifth birthday is not only a milestone for your child - but also for you as a parent. Five years full of laughter, learning, challenges and wonderful moments lie behind you.

What have you learnt in five years as a parent?

✓ **Patience is key:** children develop at their own pace.

✓ **Every child is unique:** there is no "right" or "wrong" - every child has their own path.

✓ **Mistakes are okay:** Parenting is a learning process - you're doing it just right.

✓ **Enjoy the little moments:** The first "I love you" sentence, the first self-drawn picture, the first small, independent steps - all of these make the journey as a parent so special.

📌 **Tip:** Take a moment to look back - you may want to create a photo album or write a letter to your child that they can read later.

Conclusion: Your child is now a proud preschooler!

The fifth birthday marks the end of toddlerhood and the beginning of a new chapter. Your child is now a preschooler who sees the world with new eyes and is ready for many new adventures.

💡 **What you can take away:**

✓ Your child is now more self-confident, curious and independent than ever before.

✓ The transition to preschool or school is a big step - with your support, it will be a success.

✓ The fifth birthday is a wonderful opportunity to celebrate your child and show them how special they are.

✓ You have achieved an incredible amount as a parent in the last five years - you can be proud of that!

A new chapter begins - full of adventures, new challenges and unforgettable moments. Congratulations to your child (and to you!) on five wonderful years! 🎉 🥳 🎂

29 The transition to school - A new chapter begins

Starting school is one of the biggest milestones in a child's life - and also an emotional event for parents. Your child is no longer a toddler, but a schoolchild facing new challenges: They are learning to read, write and do maths, making new friends and developing more independence.

While some children are looking forward to school, others are unsure or anxious. You may be asking yourself: **How can I best prepare my child for school? How can I support them without putting pressure on them? And what does a pre-school child really need to do well at school?**

In this chapter, you will learn how you can accompany the transition to school in a loving and playful way.

29.1 What pre-school children need for school

Parents often believe that their child needs to be able to read or do maths before they start school - but this is not necessary. Basic skills that make learning easier are much more important.

💡 **What skills are important for starting school?**

✓ **Independence:** Can get dressed, tie shoes, pack rucksack.

✓ **Social skills:** Can fit into a group, waits, listens.

✓ **Concentration:** Can concentrate on a task for 10-15 minutes.

✓ **Language skills:** Can ask questions, tell stories and understand instructions.

✓ **Fine motor skills:** Can cut with scissors, hold a pencil and trace simple shapes.

📌 **Tip:** Your child doesn't have to be able to write or do maths before starting school - it's enough if they enjoy learning and are curious.

29.2 Promoting motivation to learn without pressure

Children learn best through play - they don't need "school exercises" at home, but an environment that awakens their curiosity.

How can you encourage your child's love of learning?

✓ **Use everyday situations:** Recognising numbers in the supermarket, discovering letters on street signs.

✓ **Reading aloud:** Stories stimulate the imagination and promote vocabulary.

✓ **Incorporate movement:** Learning works better when children are allowed to move around in between.

✓ **Enable small experiences of success:** "Look, you've already written your name!"

📌 **Tip:** Pressure slows down the joy of learning - your child will still be practising enough at school, so learning should remain playful now.

29.3 How to prepare your child for everyday school life

Everyday life at school is very different from kindergarten: there are fixed timetables, rules and longer periods of concentration.

How can you prepare your child for this?

✓ **Introduce fixed routines:** Finish on time in the morning, take breaks.

✓ **Let them do tasks themselves:** Your child should practise doing things on their own.

✓ **Exercises in listening and waiting:** Games such as "I see something you don't see" encourage patience.

✓ **Arouse curiosity with positive stories about school:** "You'll learn exciting things at school!"

📌 **Tip:** The more relaxed you are about school, the more confident your child will feel.

29.4 The right school bag and initial equipment

Many children are particularly excited about starting school because they finally get their own school bag! But what does your child really need?

Checklist for school equipment:

🎒 **School bag:** Should be light, fit well and be ergonomically shaped.

✏️ **Pencil case:** With pencils, eraser, coloured pencils and a ruler.

📖 **Exercise books and folders:** Depending on school requirements (chequered, lined).

✂️ **Scissors and glue:** For handicrafts.

Change of clothes and slippers: Depending on the school for indoor use.

Lunch box and water bottle: For healthy snacks during the break.

Tip: Let your child help pick out their school supplies - this increases the anticipation!

29.5 Celebrating school enrolment: the start of a new adventure

Starting school is a special day that your child won't soon forget. Whether it's a big celebration or a small surprise - there are many ways to make the start of school an unforgettable experience.

Ideas for a lovely first day at school:

Give a school cone: Filled with little surprises (pens, erasers, a book or a small sweet).

Take souvenir photos: A photo with school bag and school cone as a memento.

A little surprise after school: A trip together or a favourite meal to start school.

Involve the family: Maybe grandma and grandpa will come to the party?

Tip: It doesn't have to be a huge party - the important thing is that your child feels special on this day.

Conclusion: A new phase of life full of opportunities

The transition to school is an important step that makes your child more independent and brings new experiences. With your support, your child will experience this change with joy and curiosity.

What you can take with you:

✓ Your child doesn't need to be able to read or do maths perfectly before starting school - social and motor skills are more important.

✓ The joy of learning comes from playful discovery, not from pressure.

✓ Everyday school life brings new routines - it helps to prepare your child for this.

✓ Good school equipment and a lovely school enrolment ceremony will make the start special.

The school years begin - a new chapter full of adventures, friendships and exciting discoveries!

30th Review and outlook - What remains and what is to come

Five years of parenthood - an exciting, challenging and wonderful journey lies behind you. Your child has taken incredible developmental steps in these years: from a helpless newborn to a curious, self-confident and inquisitive preschooler.

Maybe you're wondering: **How did the time pass so quickly? Was I a good mum or dad? Did I do everything right?** The answer is: **Yes!** Because being a parent doesn't mean perfection, but love, patience and the willingness to grow together every day.

In this chapter, we look back at the last five years and take a look at what lies ahead.

30.1 Five years of parenthood: What you have learnt

The first five years with your child were full of magical moments, but also full of challenges. You have learned to get by on little sleep, to change nappies half asleep and to be patient when your child repeats the same sentence for the tenth time.

💡 **What you have learnt as a parent in these five years:**

✓ **Patience is priceless:** children go at their own pace - and that's a good thing.

✓ **Every child is unique:** there is no "right" or "wrong" - only individual paths.

✓ **There is no such thing as perfection:** Parents make mistakes - and that's completely okay.

✓ **Small moments are the most precious:** the first words, the first smile, the first time "I love you".

📌 **Tip:** Take a moment to be proud of yourself - you've made it through five years of love and care!

30.2 Letting go and accompanying your child

At the age of five, your child will become increasingly independent. They can dress themselves, make small decisions and start to make their own friends. But even if they continue to detach themselves from you, they will still need your support.

💡 **How can you help your child grow up?**

✓ **Give them more responsibility:** Let your child take on small tasks.

✓ **Encourage them to try out new things:** Even if it fails sometimes - that's part of it.

✓ **Remain present as a safe haven:** Your child will become more independent, but will always need you close by.

✓ **Show trust:** When your child realises that you have confidence in them, they will become braver.

📌 **Tip:** Letting go doesn't mean that your child needs you less - it means that you give them the space to grow.

30.3 The next challenges in parenthood

Every age brings new challenges - and even after the first five years, there will be moments when you are in doubt or at a loss.

💡 **What comes next?**

✓ **The school years:** Your child will take on more responsibility, make new friends and experience their first challenges at school.

✓ **Stronger emotions:** Your child will become more self-confident, but also more sensitive to criticism or failure.

✓ **More independence:** Your child will become more detached from you, but at the same time will always seek your closeness.

✓ **New interests and talents:** Your child will find out what they particularly like doing - sport, music, reading or something completely different.

Tip: Stay flexible - every child develops differently and you will always find new ways to support them.

30.4 Preserving memories: Photo albums, diaries & co.

The first five years go by incredibly quickly - and it's often only later that you realise how valuable this time was. Memories are what last - they keep the special moments alive.

How can you capture the first years?

A photo album or a digital memory book: Collect the best pictures from the first five years.

A parent diary: write down funny or emotional moments - you'll love reading them later.

Videos of special milestones: First steps, first words or a particularly sweet moment.

A letter to your child: Write a letter that they can read later - about your feelings, your favourite memories and your wishes for the future.

Tip: Whether you keep a large memory book or just write down individual moments - the main thing is that you preserve the magic of those years.

30.5 Parenting - a journey that never ends

The first five years are over - but parenthood never ends. Your child will continue to grow, develop and master new challenges. Your role will change over time, but one thing will always remain the same: your child needs you - as a role model, as a listener, as a safe haven.

What is it like to be a parent?

✓ **It's an adventure:** no two days are the same.

✓ **It's challenging:** sometimes you feel overwhelmed - and that's normal.

✓ **It's unpredictable:** Children surprise you all the time.

✓ **It's the most beautiful thing in the world:** despite all the effort, there is nothing more precious than the love between parent and child.

Tip: Enjoy every phase - even if some are exhausting, they are unique and will eventually become precious memories.

Conclusion: Five years full of love, growth and unforgettable moments

Your child's first five years are over - but the journey continues. Your child is now ready for new adventures, new challenges and new learning. And you? You have given five years of love, patience and care - and will continue to do so.

What you can take with you:

✓ You have achieved an incredible amount as a parent - you can be proud of that.

✓ Your child will continue to develop - and you will accompany them lovingly.

✓ Memories are precious - keep them in pictures, letters or diaries.

✓ Parenting changes, but never stops - you will always play an important role.

No matter what the future holds - you have proven that you are a wonderful parent.
Congratulations on five wonderful years of parenthood! 🩶 ✦ 🎉

Epilogue

This book is not the work of a perfect parent - but of someone who has learnt from experience.

My name is **Alexander Gaal**, I am a pensioner and a father. I openly admit it: I did a lot of things wrong when bringing up my children. Not out of malicious intent, but out of ignorance, insecurity and the desire to do everything right. Like many parents, I was often faced with difficult decisions and only later realised which mistakes could have been avoided.

With this book, I would like to help other parents to learn from my experiences. I see it as my job not to lecture, but to offer guidance and support. **Every family is unique** and there is no perfect parenting style. But there are principles that can make life with children easier, more harmonious and happier.

As a **humanist**, I believe that we should pass on our knowledge and experience to make life easier for others. There are enough challenges in everyday life - if we support each other, we can avoid mistakes, make better decisions and guide our children with love, patience and understanding.

I hope that this book will help you to make the first five years with your child more conscious, more relaxed and happier. **Parenting is an adventure - it's not always easy, but it's the best thing life has to offer.**

All the best for you and your family!

Alexander Gaal

© 2025 Alexander Gaal
Publisher: BoD · Books on Demand GmbH, In de Tarpen 42,
22848 Norderstedt, bod@bod.de
Print: Libri Plureos GmbH, Friedensallee 273, 22763 Hamburg
ISBN: 978-3-7693-1611-7